Beyond
Darkness

Beyond Darkness

by
Jim Robertson

iUniverse, Inc.
New York   Bloomington

Beyond Darkness

Copyright © 2009 by Jim Robertson

iUniverse books may be ordered through booksellers or by contacting:

iUniverse
1663 Liberty Drive
Bloomington, IN 47403
www.iuniverse.com
1-800-Authors (1-800-288-4677)

ISBN: 978-1-4401-3122-6 (pbk)
ISBN: 978-1-4401-3123-3 (ebk)

Printed in the United States of America
iUniverse rev. date: 6/24/09

Acknowledgements

The author wants to thank the following people for helping make this book a reality.

His family: Linda McSwain Robertson, Margie Robertson Ferguson, Mark Ferguson (posthumously), Duncan Gregor Ferguson, James Robertson and Shannon Sherman Robertson

His sisters: Maureen McCarthy (posthumously), Barbara Ann Payne, Linda Jean Carruth, Sue Robertson, and Ann Somers

His brothers in law: Bill McCarthy, Robert Payne, Charles Carruth, and Jim Somers

His friends: Jerry Agent, Mallory Brooks, Carolyn and Ed Champney, Nova Corley, Ella Lou Butler Cox, Jeff and Robin Daughdrill, Sharon Evans, Judy Harrell, Georgia B. Henson, J. V. McCrory, Mary Montague, and Galand Nuchols.

Contents

Prologue

On January 20, 1960, at 7:15 a.m., I crashed my car into the side of a county dump truck and almost killed myself. No doubt the awful sound made by metal hitting metal was heard by many of the people close to the accident scene on Forest Hill Road, just on the outskirts of south Jackson, Mississippi. Probably, several of them came running to see what had happened. If so, they found what had been a good-looking Fairlane 500 Ford so badly crushed it could hardly have been recognized as a car. They would have also seen me, at the age of 20, lying on the ground. If they looked at the wreckage and then back at me, as they surely would have done, they must have said, "There's no way he could have survived that." If, in fact, those were their words, they would have been ever so close to being correct.

Considering the damage that was done to me, especially my eyes and face, there was no reason to assume I could have remained conscious long enough to provide any information about myself, but, remarkably, I did. I couldn't talk, though, until I had spat out a mouth full of blood and broken teeth. With my mouth clear, I told them my name, my daddy's name, and where we lived. As I spoke, I knew I had to act fast because I was losing my grip on consciousness. Worse yet, I thought I may be losing my grip on life.

Then, just before Mother Nature sent me into oblivion, I caught enough light to see both the earth and the sky. It's a good thing I did, too, because I would never again see them so clearly. In fact, eventually, I wouldn't even see them at all. The light would be completely gone for me and there wouldn't be anything left except darkness.

On the fateful day of my accident, I was driving to Hinds Junior College to take a final examination. It would have been the fourth and last one for that semester.

In addition to going to school, I was working the night shift at G. E.'s Jackson Lampworks. That job covered both my living expenses and my school expenses.

In many ways, my work and school situations were almost ideal, but there was one major problem that I continually faced. Regardless of my best efforts, I never got enough sleep. As a consequence, I was tired all of the time, and it was often difficult for me to stay alert.

As I tried later to figure out why my accident happened, I had to accept the idea that my fatigue could have played an important role, even very early in the morning. The driver of the dump truck said he had made every effort to prevent the crash and there is no firm evidence to refute his word. His subsequent behavior is the only thing that ever raised a question in my mind. For reasons known only to him, I suppose, he never once came to see me, nor did he make any inquiries concerning my welfare.

In the end, all that could be said was that I had been involved in a very serious accident. Its consequences were going to affect me in various ways for the rest of my entire life and knowing who was responsible wouldn't change a thing.

Chapter 1

Fighting for Life

For many hours no one could tell if I would live or if I would die. All things considered, the latter outcome seemed the most likely, but, as I came later to understand, the human spirit is difficult to extinguish. That fact explains a lot because, according to the normal laws of nature, the injuries I sustained when the hood of my car went under the side of that county dump truck were so extensive I could not have survived. A mere list of them presents a convincing case that the accident would be fatal. It reads like this – every bone in my face was broken, my nose was crushed, my sinuses were shattered, my right eye was burst, eight teeth were knocked out, my right kneecap was crushed, and my left eye sustained an undetermined amount of damage.

Since I had been continually unconscious since just after my accident, I had no way of knowing that my head had swollen to the size of a basketball and that my face was flattened. Given my condition, the experts at University Hospital, where the ambulance had taken me, decided there was no alternative but to wait until nature could make some repairs before they began their work. For my family and friends, no doubt, the wait seemed interminable. Finally, after eight days, it came to an end, and I was taken to an operating room.

Incredibly, more than ten hours were required to make all the necessary repairs. During that time, ten pints of blood had to be pumped into my body

1

to keep me alive. At times there were so many people working on me, they literally got in one another's way.

My plastic surgeon, Dr. Jim Hendricks, had the most difficult task of all. Though he didn't know what I had looked like before, he nevertheless had the responsibility of putting all those broken bones back into the right places. To help guide his hands, he got my mother, Vera Robertson, and my sister, Linda Jean, to bring him a recent portrait of me.

To reassemble all those broken bones and hold them in place, Dr. Hendricks used wire here and there and then topped off the effort by running a large pin through my face from one cheekbone to the other. He put a cork on the sharp end of that pin to prevent injury to hands that might get too close. Contrary to reason, the continuing presence of the pin did not cause pain. It did, however, irritate the skin around it and caused furious itching. I wanted very badly to reach up and scratch the itch, but for some reason I couldn't make my hands extend that far. After many futile attempts, I was finally alert enough one day to figure out what was causing all that frustration – my hands had been tied to the bed rails.

Another source of great frustration for me was the result of a tracheotomy. Obviously the procedure had been necessary to ensure my breathing, but because of its very nature, it made talking a virtual impossibility.

In addition to these frustrations, at some point I became alert enough to start worrying that people might have been killed because of what I had done. Of course, I didn't know what I had done, but I reasoned that since I was hurting all over, others might be worse off. One day after doing all that worrying for Lord knows how long, I became clear-headed enough to formulate a plan. Extending my hand as far as the rope would permit, I began making writing motions. Fortunately my sister, Linda Jean, who was with me at the time, understood my motions and put a pencil in my hand. Then she put a pad in front of me so I could put the pencil to use. For some reason, which I wondered about at the time, I wasn't really able to see the pad in front of me, but when Linda put the point of the pencil against it, I started writing anyway. We Robertsons are not known for our penmanship, but we can read most anything that has been written. The truth of that declaration was proven by Linda Jean. As soon as I finished writing, she read my words aloud. They said, "How many were killed?" To my deep relief, both she and Mama immediately assured me no life had been lost, and, in fact, I was the only one who was even injured. Thank goodness, I thought, as I sank back against the bed. Even through the haze in which I continually lived, I understood I had been given good news. I was miserable, but at least I hadn't killed anybody.

Though not many, there were other sources of comfort. Chief among them was the fact that I was given total support by my family. If I awakened from restless sleep, scared and disoriented, at least one of them was always there. Whoever was present at the time, Mama or Daddy or one of my sisters would put a kiss on my forehead or touch my arm and say, "You're all right, Jimmy." The professional nurses hired to be with me around the clock would help to meet my physical needs, but only someone who loved me could give me my much needed emotional support. When both the body and the soul are hurting, an awful lot of care is required.

Mama and Daddy set aside the bitterness of their divorce as they and my sisters soldiered on. No doubt all of them were sometimes under great pressure, but occasionally something would happen to relieve the strain.

Once, when Maureen, my oldest sister, was in my room to help me, I got her to lift my right leg with its cast from foot to hip up high in the air to a position of relative comfort. Eventually she got tired of holding it up there and when she informed me of her intention to put it back on the bed, I suggested the alternative of tying it in place. Despite all the misery she had seen, she found enough humor in my strange suggestion to laugh out loud. Perhaps I laughed a little, too, when I finally understood what a ridiculous thing I had said.

So far as I know, none of my internal organs were seriously damaged, but something obviously caused some bleeding inside my body because I eventually developed blood clots in my lungs. No one told me that was what had happened, but no one had to. One day I started coughing so violently I couldn't stop long enough to catch my breath. In moments, I was certain I was going to die. Trying every maneuver I could think of, I rose up in bed and made every possible effort to restore my breath. As usual, the nurse was there, but there was nothing she could do. It was all up to me, and I knew it. Whatever was causing the coughing had to be dislodged, and I knew that too. Though only seconds had elapsed, the pressure in my head, chest, and neck was awful, and the pain was getting so bad I could hardly stand it. The thought occurred to me that death wasn't a bad idea at all. By then I would have paid any price to stop the agony. It was hopeless though. I was strangling. There was nothing I could do except what I was doing, and that wasn't enough.

While I was coughing, my body was being thrown up and back and from side to side, but there was no position that provided any relief. As a consequence, it occurred to me that I was going to die and I actually welcomed the idea. Then, as an act of final desperation, I fell back on the bed and made one last mighty effort to clear my windpipe. To my disbelief, but more so to my immense relief, a blood clot shot through the opening where my front teeth used to be with such force that it hit the ceiling and stuck there. The wires on my remaining teeth that were used to help hold my jaws in place provided enough space for the blood clot to come flying out from my lungs. With air finally getting back in to my chest cavity, I sank against the bed and let my body begin to relax. Soon, complete exhaustion set in, and I went to sleep or, perhaps, I passed out. Whichever occurred, I barely had time to feel the nurse's hand as she took a damp cloth and wiped my mouth and face.

Evidence of the lick I had taken wasn't just in my lungs, though. It was everywhere and sometimes the pain, especially in my leg, gave new meaning to the term intense. When it became unbearable, I'd be given a shot of morphine. The relief it provided was fast and complete and deeply appreciated. If I had been asked at that time about morphine, I would have replied that it was wonderful. I would be lying in my bed hurting so badly that I was almost out of my mind just waiting until the nurse gave me my shot. Miraculously, within seconds of the time the drug was injected, I could feel it moving up my body, beginning, literally, at the tips of my toes, bringing blessed relief as it went. Typically, by the time the morphine reached my hips, I would be so relaxed I could go to sleep and, for a time, be free of that damn pain.

Apparently someone got the idea I was becoming too attached to the morphine because one day I experienced a surprising and decidedly unwanted change. I had just been given a shot that I needed very badly and was waiting for the tingle to begin, but to my dismay, after much more than enough time had elapsed, nothing was happening. In alarm bordering on desperation, I asked my nurse what was wrong. Her response was evasive, but I was able to put together enough information to conclude someone believed I was asking for shots I didn't need. In all honesty, that possibility had occurred to me too, but I had rejected it out of hand. I knew all too well that my pain was real, and I resented anyone thinking I should be denied relief from it. Though I tried over and over, I never could get used to having pain. In one word, I could describe how it made me feel – miserable.

Because of the nature of my injuries, the physician with whom I had the greatest contact was my plastic surgeon, Dr. Jim Hendricks. I could describe him in a word too – wonderful. He was one of those rare individuals who had extraordinary skills and, at the same time, great compassion. To make him even more well-rounded, he had one of the most winning personalities I had ever seen. All of this, coupled with his gentle bedside manner, always made me feel better when I got a visit from him. Sometimes he could bring a little smile to my face even with the pins still stuck in it.

One day, perhaps three weeks into my stay at the hospital, he came to see me and stayed longer than usual. In fact, he stayed long enough to tell me all manner of things about the extent of my injuries. I already had a fairly good idea about some of them. For sure, no one had to tell me my right leg had been injured nor explain to me my face had taken a severe blow, but I could tell from his demeanor, I was going to get the full picture from him whether I wanted it or not. As best I could, I tried to get prepared. If I was going to be given bad news, and I sensed that I was, I wanted to be ready for it.

I listened for changes in Dr. Hendricks' voice as he spoke, but it remained calm as he almost casually mentioned the loss of my kneecap and passed on to a description of my facial injuries. Then, pausing, as if to merely collect his thoughts, he said, "You know about your right eye, don't you?" Even though his

5

voice had betrayed no emotion, I sensed he had raised a serious matter. "What about it?" I asked, trying to maintain as much control as he was showing. "It had to be removed because it was burst," he said. I let that information sink in for a moment and thought about how I was going to be one-eyed for the rest of my life, but then my attention shifted to my remaining eye. "What about my other eye?" I asked, feeling some panic as the possibility occurred to me I might have real problems in seeing much of anything. Get ready, Jimmy, I thought to myself as I cocked my ear. Thank goodness the wait was short, and Dr. Hendricks' voice seemed unchanged as he said, "Well, we're not sure there. It was badly injured, but no one can tell yet the full extent of injury." That wasn't nearly as encouraging as what I had hoped for, so, never being one to let well enough alone, I blurted out, "I'll be able to see all right, won't I?" Once again, Dr. Hendricks's response was immediate, but his words didn't do much to slow my heart rate. All he said was, "Well, we hope so. Right now your eye is too bloodshot for us to tell." I gave him time to say more, but obviously, there was nothing else he could offer. Seconds later, he patted my arm in a friendly fashion and gave me his usual warm farewell.

After he was gone I couldn't keep my mind from returning to his words. I wanted to find something in them that would make me feel better. Try as I might, though, I couldn't come up with much. Eventually, I gave up the effort. I could tell I wasn't doing myself any good with all that thinking, besides, I was feeling awfully tired.

In actuality, I felt tired just about all the time, but that wasn't necessarily bad. For one thing, that fatigue kept me from worrying very much. In fact, except when I was hurting very badly, it kept me from doing much of anything except sleep. I would often doze off, even as I was telling myself I ought to stay awake. In all likelihood, Mother Nature knew better than I what would serve me well, but I wasn't blessed with enough wisdom to understand it then.

Perhaps my inordinate need for sleep could also explain the strange relationship I had with one of the young interns who came to see me from time to time. Maybe by an unhappy coincidence, each time he came I needed sleep much more than I needed to talk to him. Regardless of the explanation for it, our relationship got worse every time he came and, eventually, the point was reached where I hated the very idea of him being in my presence. There may have been some deep-seated psychological explanation for my attitude toward him, but at the time all I knew was that I didn't like him and I was quite sure he didn't like me either. Toward the end of my time in the hospital, our relationship deteriorated to the point where I called him a son of a bitch to his face.

Mama would have been shocked if she had heard me say those words, but Daddy would have shown little, if any, surprise. His language was pretty colorful from time to time as well. The young man didn't call me a son of a bitch in return, but I could tell he wanted to. No doubt, he was trying to be professional in his relationship with me, but his efforts weren't being successful. Consistently, we brought out the worst in one another.

As an intern, he was there to learn, and I couldn't help but wonder what he had learned from me. Maybe it was the knowledge that not all of his patients would love him

Whether he intended it or not, I also learned something from him. I learned that being a doctor doesn't necessarily make you a special person. Maybe that made us come out even. I wanted to think that anyway in later years as I would recall how I had treated him.

In spite of the unpleasantness associated with the intern and the pain and suffering I had to endure, there are many memories that have warmed my heart over the years. Friends by the scores came to my aid, and I never had an occasion to be disappointed in them. Often I was only vaguely aware of what they were doing, but, at other times, I knew exactly what was happening. I remember, for example, a visit from my childhood friend, Frank Jones, and his brother, Bob. They drove up from Liberty together and stood at my bedside a long time talking with me.

I also remember Scottie Graham and Virginia Slaughter, friends from G. E., coming into my room and hugging me and telling me how sorry they were that I had been hurt. Other friends from G. E. and from Byram Methodist Church, where I was a member for a time, also donated enough blood to cover all my needs. That meant I didn't have to pay a dime for the ten pints that were used to keep me alive.

Friends from all over Amite County who came to the barber shop made up a collection and sent it to me to help cover my hospital costs. Those same friends and many others also continually kept me in their prayers.

With all the help I got, I made it through one day and then another until I was finally told I could go home. When I was discharged, I had been in the hospital for a total of 27 days. However, since I had been either unconscious or only semiconscious for most of that time, 27 days had very little meaning for me.

Time and other factors have erased most of the memories of what occurred on the day of my discharge, but a few things stayed with me. I remember, for example, being taken out to Daddy's car in a wheelchair with my right leg being propped up out of the way. Daddy and my stepmother, Lucille, walked on each side of the wheelchair just to be sure, I supposed.

I was put on the backseat of the car with my right leg turned out to the side. The ride to Daddy's and Lucille's home, my second home, would have taken only about 20 minutes, but it seemed like a long time to me.

When we got to the house and started trying to figure out the best way to get me inside, I was the one who settled the issue. At my suggestion, Daddy got on my right side because that's where I needed the greatest support, and Lucille got on my left. With me having an arm over the shoulder of each of them, getting inside the house didn't prove to be very difficult. Even so, the effort still tired me out.

As I lay down on the bed I had left 27 and a half days before, I was conscious of the fact that I was a different person in many ways. For one thing, even with a cast on my leg, I weighed only 108 pounds. With me being so diminished, it's no wonder that my sister, Sue, upon seeing me that afternoon when she came in from school, didn't know who I was.

Chapter 2

Home and Family

At the time of my accident I'd only been away from my home in Liberty, Mississippi, a little over two and a half years. Even so, I think I made a good adjustment to not being around the people of Amite County who had known me all my life and, the best I could tell, felt a certain obligation to assure I was doing all right. As I was to eventually understand, those same people, both family and friends, had taught me a set of values that would be tested many times and not be found wanting. They must have known that sometimes I wouldn't get the message just by watching them because they would look me in the eye and tell me quite explicitly what they felt was important. Quite naturally, that kind of teaching occurred in church and school regularly, but occasionally it would occur in places you wouldn't even think about.

The one who taught the most, of course, was Mama. I could make a long list of the values she instilled in me, but the one that stands out above all the rest is honesty. It was so much a part of who Mama was that I rarely think about her without also thinking about it. Mama would tell you the truth. You could count on that as surely as you could count on anything. It was a standard she lived by every day. Those of us who were fortunate enough to be in her family were expected to meet that standard as well. In one way or another, Mama is a part of all my childhood memories.

For much of my childhood there is also a close association with the courthouse square, known simply as the Court Square. For various reasons, not the least of which was that it was located just across the street from where I lived, the Court Square was my playground. Until the age of twelve when I started working regularly, I spent many hours virtually every week playing with my friends in the open spaces it provided. Though many playmates came and went, Garland Hutto, Malcolm Swearingen, and Bobby Walsh showed up most often and stayed the longest.

For the first eight years of my life, Daddy was Amite County's Superintendent of Education and, as a consequence, had an office in the courthouse. If he chose to do so he could look out his window and see my friends and me playing on the Court Square. Sometimes my sisters Barbara Ann and Linda Jean would be playing out there too, but we boys didn't normally have girls participating in our games which I think was fine with them.

My great-uncle, John H. Parker, was also in the courthouse during that time serving as Chancery Clerk, but his office was in the back of the building. I went by to see him once in a while, but he stayed pretty busy and I never had the feeling he wanted me around very much. I knew he loved me, of course. He showed that by the way he smiled and ruffled my hair when I stopped by. Lots of times what I really wanted was for him to give me a nickel so I could buy a Coke, but that idea didn't seem to occur to him very often. My oldest sister, Maureen, would think of it once in a while though, when she had a part-time job working for him.

In my early years, we almost never left town except to visit Daddy's family in the Homochitto community. My older Robertson cousins, such as Jimmy Carol, Reggie, and Joseph were always present as was our cousin Howell "Sonny" Huff, and I got to watch as they did the things bigger and older boys could do. Sometimes Kenneth and Lannis were there too, but not often. My girl cousins such as Jennifer, Sherry, and sometimes Alice would be around, but, of course, a boy didn't play with them.

My grandfather, Jim Robertson, always held a special place in Daddy's heart and most everybody else's, as far as I could tell, but since he never paid me any attention I had no relationship with him. He mostly ignored my sisters and Mama as well, something I never understood, but I guess Daddy didn't notice.

Sometimes we went to Mama's old home, too, but that was always just for part of a day. My great-uncles Malone and Davis, both bachelors, lived in the house where Mama was reared, and she would return to it anytime she had a chance. My uncles Malone and Davis were no better with kids than their brother John H., but being around them was still enjoyable. They were great storytellers, and Uncle Davis had a very sweet disposition. Uncle Malone ran a store and this made him important to everybody. There were other uncles too such as Lem, Carey, and Tom, but for various reasons we didn't see them much.

When I was seven, Daddy did a memorable thing for all of us, even Mama. What he did was to take us to Baton Rouge to see Gene Autry. There may have been a question in the minds of some people as to who was the real king of the cowboys, but once I had seen Gene Autry in person the issue was settled for me. Roy Rogers didn't have a chance.

Gene could ride a horse better than anybody and that horse was something to behold. After all, he was named Champ. We watched in absolute amazement as Gene got Champ to do all manner of fascinating things including giving us a polite bow at the end of his performance and then walking backwards as he and his master left the arena while we cheered and clapped.

As if seeing Gene Autry and Champ wasn't enough to last a lifetime, the next year Daddy took us to the gulf coast to spend several days with the Moore family. While Mama watched from the seawall, Barbara Ann, Linda Jean, and I had the great privilege of riding in a sailboat. Soon after we got started I made the boat skipper mad because I failed to get out of the way of the boom when it changed directions too fast for me, but I tried to not let that bother me. Thinking about it sixty years later I can almost feel the wind in my face while Linda Jean got under the seat so she wouldn't blister, and Barbara Ann sat there smiling with her hand over the side to touch the water.

The next day when we went fishing I caught a speckled trout, which Daddy declared to be the best fish in the entire ocean. It seemed to be real big when I finally got it into the boat, but I noticed that night at supper the entire fish fit on my plate with room to spare. Boy was it good, though. Of course it would have been; after all, it was the finest fish there was.

Three years later in the summer of '51, Daddy did something else I never forgot, but ten thousand times over I wished I could. At first I thought what he had done was great because he let us spend the entire summer in Jackson. It wasn't until we had gotten back home that I learned he had taken all of us up there for a purpose that was so terrible I had no words to describe it. Barbara Ann, Linda Jean, and I had been tricked into believing we were on a summer-long vacation, but that wasn't it at all.

Before I hardly knew what had happened, when we got home Daddy brought in our things and then left. Or, as I was to think to myself only a few minutes later, the selfish son of a bitch walked out of our lives, got in his car and drove away. It was what Mama had to share with us that caused me to have such terrible thoughts about my Daddy. As soon as he was out of sight, Mama called us together and, with tears in her eyes, said, "Children, your Daddy has left us." Tears came into my eyes too as I sprang up and said, "Why didn't you tell us he was going to leave us?" "What good would it have done?" Mama asked in a voice somewhere between sorrow and anger. "Maybe I could have stopped him," I said. "Well, you couldn't," Mama said as Linda Jean started crying and crawled up into Mama's lap. Barbara Ann went back to her room, to cry alone I suppose.

For years Daddy often left for various reasons, but we always knew he would be back home soon where he was supposed to be. When he left at the end of that summer we knew nothing would ever be the same. An uneasy feeling crept into me and stayed there. For many years I could keep it at bay most of the time, but every now and then something would happen such as a father and son banquet, and the feeling would return full force. I did not believe my Daddy loved me. If he did, he never could have left me. It didn't matter how many times he told me by phone that I was precious to him.

In the days following Daddy's departure, I gradually came to understand what had happened that summer of '51. Daddy had finally gotten the divorce he had been planning to get for some time. Mama had not wanted him to divorce her for a host of reasons, but I don't believe her personal happiness was one of them. Regardless of what lay behind her opposition, she was firm in it and even got Maureen to fly down from Columbia, South Carolina, where she and her new husband, Bill McCarthy, were living, to try to talk Daddy into changing his mind. If anyone could have done that it was Maureen. Her position as the firstborn child and especially being pregnant at the time gave her a status no one else had, but it still wasn't enough. As people in our family would say, "Daddy was hell-bent on getting that divorce, and nothing would stop him." He said he wanted his freedom and that there wasn't another woman, but that must not have been the truth. Within a few months he was married to Lucille Hutchinson, a woman only a few years older than Maureen. They setup housekeeping in Jackson, and soon my sister Sue was born.

Divorce in Mississippi in 1951, especially Amite County, was so rare I'd only heard of it happening. I didn't know a single person who'd ever gotten one until my Daddy got his. I wasn't merely the only boy in my class whose Daddy had divorced his mother, as far as I knew I was the only boy in the entire school who fit that description. I hated that fact, too, because up until then my school experiences had generally been far from unpleasant. The first grade had been fairly difficult for me, largely because of my maturity I think, but after that, things had improved substantially.

From the second grade on I think I came into my own year by year, and by the fifth grade, if someone had asked how I felt about school, I would have said I liked it. Mrs. Alice Melton was my teacher in the fifth grade and that fact alone largely explains why I felt the way I did. With her virtually everything took on a positive character. I don't remember a single reprimand ever coming from her. She treated me and all of her students with respect, and I believe we all loved her. I certainly did, and when I think of her I always get a warm feeling inside. I considered myself fortunate to have had her as a teacher and to my everlasting satisfaction, I was able to tell her that many times and in many ways before cancer stole her away.

It was also in the fifth grade when I established myself as a championship speller. In fact, as I recall it, I was the best speller in the entire class. For some reason, however, Sharon Byrd Terrell and Gayle Harvey Van Norman remember this matter somewhat differently.

From the seventh grade on, of course, I had to deal with school and the rest of life for that matter, largely without Daddy's help. He occasionally called me on the phone, and one time he even wrote me a letter. That was about it for a very long time, but Mama was always there as were my sisters Barbara Ann and Linda Jean. Maureen spent time with us, too, when she could, coming home for visits with her husband Bill. In fact from March until October of '52 and again from February until May of '53, Maureen and her baby, Billy, lived with us while Bill fulfilled his military obligations and then completed his master's degree.

I also had the benefit of excellent role models especially from Liberty's churches. From the Methodist Church, which I had attended as far back as I could remember, I had Ray Martin, numbers of Smiths and Terrells, Mrs. Marguerite Felder, the Bells, Butlers, and Bristers and others who came and went. Sunday school on Sunday morning and MYF in the evening made the Sabbath a special day in my life. From time to time I also had the great thrill of riding in Mrs. Lottie Terrell's bus to MYF sub-district meetings in what seemed like faraway places.

As a teenager I started going to the Baptist church with Mama. I found good role models for myself there, too. Charles Causey taught me the value of humility, and I learned other important lessons from Zelma Rae Cruise, Percy Hazlewood, the Walshes, and Louis Marsalis.

Though I never belonged to either the Presbyterian or the Mormon churches, both of them supplied me with good examples to follow. The pillars of the Presbyterian Church included the Jacksons, McGehees, Gordons, Nunnerys, Strattons, and Causeys. The Blalocks and their various connections accounted for most of the membership of the Mormon Church. All of them numbered among my friends and acquaintances, but Walter Blalock played a very special role in my life as the leader of my Boy Scout troop.

Through necessity if not through choice, for several years after Daddy left, Mama, my sisters, and I stayed very close to home. The principle reason for us doing so little traveling was that we didn't have a car. When we wanted to go somewhere we either walked or caught a ride with someone. I was well aware there were many other people who had this limitation, but I still hated it and longed for the day when I could own a car. It was a terrible inconvenience for Mama and my sisters too, especially in bad weather. Mama hated the cold, and I always felt badly when she had to get out in it. That was regularly the case though, because it wasn't long after Daddy left that Mama took a full-time job as a clerk in the M & T Store. I guess she had to for us to make ends meet. The money Daddy sent every month just wasn't enough.

I started working regularly on Saturdays about the same time Mama took her job. Mr. Sonny Quin and Mrs. Lola Tumey could often put me to use bagging groceries and doing the countless other things required to make a business run smoothly. My day began at 7 a.m. and didn't end until the last customer had left town, sometimes as late as 10 p.m. My starting pay was $3, and I'm sure I earned every cent of it. Mama, of course, worked long hours too, and kept our home going as well. What a lady.

The summer I was thirteen I filled in for my good buddy Garland Hutto as a shoeshine boy in the barbershop. He had what I believed to be the unbelievably wonderful opportunity of going all the way out to Cimarron, New Mexico, to stay at the Philmont Scout Ranch. After that I worked for him several other times, and he did me additional favors as well. In 1960, however, he did something so extraordinary I have had many occasions to marvel at the depth of his friendship. What he did was to offer me one of his eyes. Like many people at the time, he had the mistaken idea an eye from another person could help me, and because he wanted very badly to do that, he made his exquisite offer. In the years since then, I've been given many gifts that were special, even precious, but never one quite so touching.

With money always being in short supply, I felt that I should take advantage of any work opportunity that presented itself. Thus, when I learned that Mr. and Mrs. Dougall needed a boy to work before and after school and all day Saturday at their Western Auto store, I applied for the job in person and, happily, was selected for it. At seven o'clock each morning, I cleaned the store and on cold days lit an old kerosene furnace that heated the building. At other times I performed such chores as putting up stock, running errands, and serving as a clerk when needed. The Dougalls paid me $8 per week for my services, minus the 16¢ held out for Social Security.

I kept the Western Auto job until the summer between my junior and senior years. Daddy offered me the opportunity to work for him and Lucille on the new home they planned to build. He agreed to provide me with room and board and pay me an hourly wage of 65¢. Having no better offers, I took it. My relationship with Daddy was still strained, and I felt ambivalent, at best, toward Lucille, but I still decided to spend that summer with them and my sister Sue, whom I scarcely knew. Before the summer of '56 I had spent very little time with Daddy, Lucille, and Sue. I had been with them for a week when I had a hernia corrected and for an additional three days when T. F. Badon gave me the great privilege of serving as a page in the Mississippi House of Representatives, but that was about it.

The summer of '56 proved to be a good one for me. I sharpened the carpentry skills Mr. Ray Martin had taught me in shop and found that my hands almost always knew what to do when a construction problem presented itself. Daddy and I improved our relationship some, but for me it was still an uneasy one in many regards. I couldn't feel completely comfortable with Lucille because of her role in Daddy's divorce, but Sue and I got along splendidly.

More importantly for me at the time, I learned that a pretty good number of attractive young girls in and around Jackson felt disposed to spend some of their time with me, and I was happy to accommodate them every chance I got. To his credit, Daddy was understanding about these activities and even gave me use of his sleek '51 Studebaker to enable me to expand my circle of friends. Those friends, especially the girls, helped me develop a positive self-image. Through their eyes I began to see myself in a different light, and I liked what I saw.

Late in that summer of '56 I also realized a dream of several years standing. I bought a car. Though it was a largely worn-out 1953 six-cylinder Ford, in my mind it had the quality and the character of a brand new Cadillac. If it had been made of gold, it would not have been any more precious.

When I returned home at the end of the summer to finish my last year of high school, I had to find a job that would provide me with enough income to make my monthly car payment and, hopefully, have a little something left over. My options were few. In fact they were virtually nonexistent, and I'd almost reached the point of panic before I learned that the *Times Picayune* paper route was up for grabs. Wasting no time, I made the necessary contacts in New Orleans and succeeded in my efforts to get the route assigned to me.

I took my new job with high hopes, but it wasn't long before I knew most of them wouldn't be realized. In fact, all in all, it was the worst job I ever had. Among other problems associated with it, I quickly discovered there was no way I could finish my work early enough to get to school on time unless I had someone to help me. In solving that problem by hiring a young black boy named Pete to be my assistant, I suffered a significant reduction in my net profit. Having no other choice, however, I kept the route until I graduated. At least, I told myself when I could finally give it up, I hadn't missed a car payment.

When I looked back at the six years I spent finishing grades seven through twelve, I could feel some pride for what I had accomplished, but there were also plenty of regrets. Typically my performance in class was merely average and, occasionally, not even that high. My classmates seemed to like me fairly well, but I doubt seriously that many of my teachers could have said, in truth, that they held me in high regard. Other than Miss Zelma Rae Cruise who always thought I was as cute as a button, my teachers probably felt their lives would have been easier if I had been somewhere else. Somewhat regularly, my behavior in class was something less than exemplary.

Things finally came to a head one day in the fall of my senior year. Mr. Dallas Stevenson, under whom I was taking Government, obviously had reached the end of his patience with me. He stopped me on campus so we could have a little talk. He hailed me as I left the lunchroom and deliberately put his one good arm around me. With me securely within his embrace, he pulled me close and said, "Boy, what's the matter with you?" What he did was a surprise to me, but as I looked into his eyes, I knew his actions were motivated by deep concern for me, perhaps even love, and so I had no alternative but to tell him the truth. I let him know what it was like to be in my shoes, and as I spoke I could see he understood. In fact, when I finished telling him about how Daddy had hurt me, he told me he knew it was so but I had to remember that plenty people cared for me deeply and I was going to have to stop letting them down.

I can't say that Mr. Stevenson caused me to immediately turn things around, but I can say I did make some improvements and, as the end of my senior year approached, I was doing reasonably well. Mr. Fred LeBlanc and Mrs. Jean Walsh gave me a nice role in our class play, and both my attitude toward school and my performance were continually improving. Quite happily, my classmates and I rounded out our school experience by taking a trip to Panama City, Florida, by far the farthest from home that I'd ever been.

Years later I entertained many audiences by telling them in mock seriousness that I was still mad at Ella Lou Butler for keeping me from being valedictorian of our class of 50 students. And after just the right pause I would say, "Of course, if she hadn't kept me from being valedictorian, there were 27 others who would have."

When we finished our school year in mid-April of 1957, like a lot of my fellow graduates, I went to Baton Rouge in search of employment. Barbara Ann and her husband, Robert Payne, had been living there since soon after their marriage in '53, so I had a good place to stay and a chance to visit with my young nephew Bobby. Sadly, their first child, Cherrie, had been born prematurely and only lived a few weeks. Happily, however, Barbara was pregnant at the time of my visit, and several months later gave birth to a second daughter, Janice. Two years later she and Robert rounded out their family by having a second son, Larry.

I gave the idea of working in Baton Rouge my best shot, but it was to no avail. Daddy had good luck on my behalf, however, so after an unproductive week I left Baton Rouge for Jackson.

The job that awaited me was helping to take inventory at University Hospital at a wage of 75¢ an hour. That work played out after a few weeks, but right on its heels I found a job working in a cold storage plant. Like my paper route, that was a terrible job. I never did feel comfortable being closed up in a large freezer wondering the whole time how I would get out of there if something happened. There were, however, two good things about that job. First, it paid me 25¢ an hour more than the previous one and, secondly, it didn't last very long. At the end of the summer I was able to tell Southern United Ice Company good bye as I continued my education at Hinds Junior College.

In effect, Daddy had chosen Hinds for me, but I didn't object since I knew it was a good choice. The campus was small, and, within a short period of time, I had a circle of friends and had gotten to know several faculty members. In fact one of them, Miss Lurlene Stewart, was from southwest Mississippi. Another of them, Mrs. Jobie Harris, was an old friend of Daddy's, as was the president of the college, George McLendon. Though my friend, Wayne Boyd, had to pay an out-of-district fee for the privilege of going to Hinds, he accompanied me up there because of the college's fine music program. Quite naturally we roomed together, and he too made a nice adjustment to our new environment.

Following my usual school pattern, I did only fairly well both my first and second semesters, so I decided to sit out the first semester of the following school year. During the summer of '58, I worked for six weeks as a calf scaler for Swift Packing Company followed by a stint as a service station attendant.

When school started again in January of '59, I decided to take a few classes in the evening. I secured fairly decent employment with General Electric Lampworks, helping to make both 40- and 20-watt fluorescent lights. My shift began at 6:15 a.m. and ended at 2:45 p.m., giving me plenty of time to take night classes. Daddy had paid for my initial college work, but I elected to be independent thereafter. I signed up for three classes, and though I technically might not have been eligible to stay in the dormitory, I did so anyway. The fact that Daddy and the Dean of Men were longtime friends may have had something to do with it, but I didn't ask any questions.

Being willing to work a full day at a physically demanding job and then take classes at night suggested that I had reached a fairly high level of maturity. My actual performance, however, didn't even come close to supporting such an observation. In fact, I barely passed two out of the three classes I took. I did, however, improve my personality quite a little bit. My friend Jimmy Simmons was still at Hinds, making it possible for us to resume the very pleasant association we had begun the previous year. My old roommate, Wayne Boyd, didn't return for a second year, and another good friend, Adolphus Moore, dropped out after getting married. Jimmy and I carried on without them, however, and we went out together with as many different girls as we could manage. I found this to be a very pleasant way of improving my personality, and Jimmy was happy to add any assistance he could. By the end of the semester, a lot of pretty girls had been treated to the pleasure of our company.

I took the summer of '59 off from college, and when GE closed down for two weeks so all of its employees could have some time off, I took Mama and Linda Jean on a short Florida vacation. Visiting the Sunshine State with my graduating class had been such a good experience for me, I had hopes they might enjoy it as well.

With Linda Jean helping me with some of the driving, we easily made it to Pensacola in one day, seeing various interesting sights along the way, especially in Mobile. Going through the tunnel, however, seemed a little tight for all of us.

My original plan was for us to go as far down as Panama City. That didn't prove to be necessary. We had a nice visit in Pensacola and then drove back to the Mississippi gulf coast and spent a night there before returning home to Liberty.

I had moved in with Daddy, Lucille, Sue, and, by then, baby sister Ann when the dorm closed, and it seemed to be working out so well I decided to stay on for a while. Sensing a little resistance on Daddy's part, however, I insisted on paying rent. That probably didn't mollify him completely, but at least it made me feel somewhat more independent.

As always Lucille was very tolerant of me, and for the most part, she and I got along fine. As soon as school started, however, I didn't see much of her or anyone else in the family except at breakfast and on weekends. Every weekday was long and full for me since my classes in Raymond, 15 miles away, began at 8:00 a.m. and didn't end until almost time for me to begin my GE work shift at 2:45 p.m. Since the shift didn't end until 11:15 p.m, I almost never got to bed before midnight. As a result, I was always tired.

I got to sleep in most every Sunday and occasionally on Saturday, but Daddy very often needed me to help him do something. He was a very smart man but almost incompetent when it came to using his hands unless the work was related to farming. He loved the soil and could grow almost anything. I was involved in virtually all of his projects, and, to his credit, he could come up with a lot of ideas. I guess it never occurred to him that I had plenty to do without having to help him. It also occurs to me, though, that I never thought to tell him that I didn't really have either the time or the energy for everything he had in mind. Actually, even if I had entertained such an idea, I probably wouldn't have brought it up. Daddy liked for things to be done his way.

Despite all the things I had to do, I actually performed fairly well in school that semester. In fact, that thought occurred to me as I headed for Raymond on that cold morning on January 20, 1960.

Considering what happened that day, my life would have been quite different if I had decided to do something else. Perhaps I would have been better off if I had never even left Amite County in the first place. After all, it was my home and, as I said later in a poem, "That's where my heart still abides."

Chapter 3

Trying to Get Well

Since Lucille was a nurse, she probably knew I had contracted a staph infection while I was in the hospital, but I wasn't aware of it until later. Having previously never even heard of that infection, I initially thought the term for it was "staff," meaning it was passed from the hospital staff. Of course, I finally came to understand that s-t-a-p-h is short for Staphylococcus and that once you have the infection in your body, getting rid of it can present some real difficulties. That is especially true for anyone already in a weakened condition. I wound up having it for a year, and before I finally got rid of it, it had caused me a great deal of suffering and substantially delayed the time required for my full recovery from the accident.

My first awareness of the staph infection occurred when my leg cast was removed. Lucille had taken me back to University Hospital for that procedure. From the way my knee felt, I was pretty sure it was completely well, and that proved to be the case. I felt some elation over that discovery because it meant I could give up the crutches they'd been insisting I use.

Though probably routine from a medical perspective the removal of the cast was very interesting to me. It was literally sawed off my leg, and to this day I remember the buzzing sound made by the blade as it cut through the plaster. I also recall the pleasant feel of the cool air on my skin as the cast fell away and exposed it.

The best I could tell, everything was routine until the part of the cast that had covered half of my leg was removed. Quite unexpectedly, when it came off, a good portion of my flesh went with it. Perhaps the cast had been a little too tight or, maybe, I had a pressure wound from being in the same position for too long a period of time. Whatever the cause, the result was that a substantial portion of the calf of my leg had wasted away, and the evidence of that loss would always remain.

In succeeding days, my staph infection seemed to center itself in my calf wound. The presence of the infection prevented the wound from healing properly, and it caused my calf muscles to contract. When that occurred, the end of my foot was pulled downward and walking on it became almost impossible. I knew I couldn't permit that to happen, so I devised a system of my own to reverse the contractions. Very deliberately as I lay in bed, I put the ball of my foot against the footboard and applied enough pressure to force my calf muscle to stretch. I caused myself pain with this exercise, but the improvements I could detect were enough to keep me at it for the long haul. In fact, I didn't quit until I'd stretched my muscles back to their normal length. My right leg was too badly damaged to ever be as strong as the left, but at least I'd be able to walk on it.

Much of the credit for improvements in the condition of my right leg also goes to Ben Piazza and the rehabilitation department at University Hospital. The whirlpool, massages, and other techniques designed to strengthen my leg and assure its continued viability were, on the whole, quite successful. As a result, the absence of my kneecap never presented a serious problem.

Though it took a couple of months for the evidence to manifest itself, in addition to the staph settling in the calf of my leg, it also settled in my nasal passages and sinuses. As a consequence, I didn't breathe properly through my nose for months on end, and my sense of smell was virtually destroyed.

Eventually the infection caused me a great deal of pain despite all those hot packs applied by Barbara Ann and Linda Jean. Nature being what it is, the pressure that built up from the damage being done by the staph infection had defined a release and that release came finally from fluids being forced through both the inside and outside of my right cheek. That process, of course, took weeks, and the continuing swelling of my face during that time caused such severe pain, the drugs I was taking could provide little help for me. At times, it felt as if my right cheek was going to burst. Eventually, that was essentially what happened. A hole was formed both inside my cheek and outside, which permitted drainage and relief from some of the pressure but did not permanently cure the problem. The cure came ten months later when I was finally given a drug that was able to kill the infection.

Until I was rid of it, the staph infection caused problems for various parts of my body. I dealt with them as well as I could, but they would often wear me down, and, worse yet, the infection delayed my recovery for many months. Quite naturally the quality of my life suffered every second of that time.

In addition to struggling with the staph infection, I had other problems as well. One of them, my empty eye socket, was hard for me to handle. The idea of me having an artificial eye, called an ophthalmological prosthesis, was an assault on my ego, but I knew I had no alternative. Accordingly, I got Maureen to take me to Mississippi Optical, which, according to my ophthalmologist, provided that service.

A nice man named Jimmy Stubblefield worked with me and eventually fitted me with what seemed to be an acceptable prosthesis. The whole process was pretty simple because all he had to do was to find one already made that was the right shape, size, and color to meet my needs.

When Mr. Stubblefield finished his work, I assumed, naively as it turned out, that his work would serve me well. Support for that assumption was provided by a couple of buddies of mine from G.E., Cliff Dent and Martin Holloway, who, upon seeing me with my new prosthesis for the first time, declared that I "Looked pretty good," and no one else offered a contrary opinion.

Mid summer, however, an ophthalmologist in Little Rock gave me a decidedly different impression. Mincing no words whatever, he said that the prosthesis neither looked good nor fit well. Seeing my dismay, he directed me to an expert who, after a few visits, fitted me with a tailor-made prosthesis that I used quite satisfactorily for ten years.

Within six weeks of my release from the hospital, I also learned that my jaws had healed enough for the wires holding them in place to be removed. That would mean I could, once again, eat what I wanted to, and the prospect of that freedom lifted my spirits higher than they'd been in quite a while. I knew what my first meal was going to be when the wires came out. I was going to have an oyster supper, and I planned to eat as many of them as I could hold.

I was staying with Maureen and family when the much anticipated day finally arrived. Knowing it was a very special occasion, my brother-in-law, Bill, asked what I'd like to have for my first meal. When I told him oysters, he said he'd be honored to be the one to cook them.

I got the wires out on a Monday afternoon, and with his usual military precision, Bill had everything ready at precisely 6:00 when he came to my room to assist me to the table. My mouth started watering as soon as I sat down, but good Catholics as they were, not a bite could be taken until the Lord was reassured of our thankfulness.

In my mind, I was poised for action and as soon as I heard the word "Amen," I stabbed an oyster and brought it up to my mouth. It was my plan to lay it on tongue and just let it sit there for a while. Then, slowly, I was going to bite into it and let its succulent juices flow throughout my mouth.

Virtually the second the oyster touched my lips, however, I knew I was in trouble. Regardless of how I turned my fork, I couldn't get the oyster to go into my mouth. With each new effort, my level of frustration escalated. Damn, I thought. I spent all that time looking forward to this meal, but now I can't eat it.

I laid my fork down and put my right hand up to my mouth to confirm what I knew by then I was going to find. As I expected, when I touched both an upper and a lower tooth while flexing my jaw muscles, there was no discernable movement. In disbelief and in disappointment, I tried to force my mouth open with my thumb and fingers, but it was impossible. Even when I pressed hard enough against my upper and lower teeth to cause pain, there was no movement. Why in hell, I asked myself in frustration, are all these things happening to me?

By then Maureen and Bill had figured out what had occurred, and they quickly began to tell me that it wouldn't be long before I'd be able to open my mouth normally and eat just as I'd always done. I believed them, of course, but right then their words didn't provide much consolation. A plate of oysters lay before me, and I wanted desperately to eat them. The fact that I couldn't made me feel helpless. If my nephew, Billy, and nieces, Lynn and Mary, had not been there, I think I would have cried. They were sensitive children, however, so I wouldn't let myself upset them.

As Maureen and Bill had predicted, my jaw muscles limbered up a few days later, enabling me to eat normally, and soon after that I started seeing the dentist Daddy and Lucille had chosen as the one to fit me with bridges. I was anxious to get this done because I knew I looked awful with eight teeth missing in the front of my mouth. Obviously, I had held on to my vanity despite my various other losses.

Considering the level of dental sophistication at the time, my bridges were well done. The only noticeable problem I ever experienced was that they didn't meet precisely enough to permit me to bite through a thin leaf of lettuce. Otherwise everything was fine, and everyone seemed to be pleased with the way my bridges looked in my mouth. Before my accident, a lot of the women at G.E. would look at me as I gave them a smile, showing as many of my teeth as I could, and say, "Hello there, pretty boy." I remembered those occasions fondly, and for days after I was fitted with my bridges, I would run my tongue over them and wonder if those women would give me that same greeting again.

Chapter 4

The Light Goes Out

Every time progress was made in restoring my body to some semblance of normal, a little hope would also be restored. Sometimes that hope would be strong enough to sustain me for several days in succession, but I was never completely at ease. In the back of my mind there was always the memory of Dr. Hendricks telling me about his uncertainty concerning the condition of my left eye. Especially during those periods when I was relatively free of pain and able to think clearly, I would wonder about that eye and, fairly often, that wonder would turn to fear. When I couldn't control the thought that I was going to be blind, the fear would turn into terror. I had seen blind people before, and I didn't think I could stand to be like that. In my mind, nothing was as important as being able to see.

On a good day I could almost convince myself that things were going to turn out OK because a little of my vision was returning. My body was absorbing some of the blood clots in my eye, and as that occurred I began to see more than simply shadows. Within a month of my release from the hospital, I could distinguish shapes, but it always seemed as if I was seeing things through a deep fog. Since we often had cloudy days at that time of year, however, it wasn't too great a stretch for me to think that the weather was at least partially responsible.

In succeeding days, my vision improved even more, and I reached the point where I could distinguish colors. They weren't as sharp and clear as I would have liked, but at least they were there. For some reason, however, I couldn't see anything in the center of my eye. Everything was off to the side. Being unable to bring objects into focus was frustrating of course, but, as I told myself, at least I was seeing, and that was a hell of a lot better than not seeing.

The light in my bathroom was strong and I'm quite sure the mirror over my lavatory caught a clear image of me each time I passed in front of it. But I didn't try to see what I looked like. No one had told me I would be shocked by my appearance but subconsciously I probably feared that I would. Perhaps all I wanted was the memory of myself as a good-looking young man with pretty green eyes, straight white teeth, and a ready smile.

One morning, a few days after I had begun to feel good about the way things had started going for me, Daddy came in and awakened me by opening my curtains. I heard the distinctive sound they made as he pulled the drawstring. Turning toward the window, I said. "Why is it so dark today?" Quickly, with his voice taking on an unusual tone, Daddy said, "It's not, the sun is out and the day is as bright as it can be." Oh God, I thought, as I opened my eyes as wide as they would go and turned toward Daddy's voice. I could see nothing, not even a shadow. Without thinking what it might do to Daddy, I cried out, "I can't see anything." A thousand thoughts flew through my mind as I waited for Daddy to say something. It must have been hard for him to get himself under control because the silence dragged out a good while. Finally he leaned over and rubbed my shoulder and said, "Buddy, let's not worry about this. We'll go see your ophthalmologist after breakfast and let him tell us what is going on." If Daddy had believed I was going to follow his suggestion, he would have been wrong. As soon as he left my room and I was alone, I started to worry. I just couldn't keep myself from it. Thoughts flashed through my mind at lightning speed, and every one of them made me feel anxious. Over and over I asked myself what on earth I was going to do if I was blind. It occurred to me that, in many ways, my life would be over if I couldn't see. And, fleetingly, I even wondered if I wanted to live in a world of darkness.

God, I'm miserable, I thought over and over. I remembered all of the bad things that had happened to me in recent weeks and wondered if I had the strength to stand yet another. I was feeling sorry for myself, and I knew it. But, I couldn't stop it. As I wallowed in my self pity, I kept thinking over and over that there was no hope that I could ever be the person I used to be. Then, realizing that hope was dead, I sank even lower into depression.

Thank goodness it wasn't long before Daddy returned with my breakfast. Even though I had only been alone for about fifteen minutes, it had seemed like an eternity. After putting my plate in the same place as always, Daddy informed me with obvious pleasure in his voice that I was going to have flapjacks and bacon. Then, still acting as if nothing was different, he said he would be back to see me after he had talked with Dr. Hughes.

I continued to lie in my bed for a moment after Daddy left. Two thoughts occurred to me in rapid succession with the second one catching me by surprise. First, I recognized the fact that I was still miserable, but secondly, despite my misery, I realized I was hungry. Under other circumstances, that realization would have brought a smile to my face. That was what I was thinking as I moved from the bed to the table.

Finding everything exactly as I knew it would be, I picked up my fork and started eating. Steadily moving my hand from plate to mouth, I didn't let myself dwell on the fact that I was doing everything by touch. Occasionally, I stopped eating long enough to lick a little syrup off my fingers, not because I had to but because I wanted to. I knew Emily Post wouldn't have approved but then what would she have known about the way you're supposed to eat flapjacks.

When I finished my meal I went to the bathroom and brushed my teeth. Brushing after every meal had always been my routine and I wasn't about to change it especially that morning with my teeth coated with sugar. As I stood before the mirror, in which I could not see myself, I forced my attention on the job at hand. Right then that was what was important to me. Who knew what would be important later.

I'd been back in my room only a few minutes before Daddy came in to tell me I had less than an hour before my appointment with Dr. Hughes. Knowing I couldn't go anywhere without getting cleaned up, I rolled out of bed, slipped off my pajamas, and went straight to the shower. Setting the control as hot as I could stand it, I stood there and let the water beat down on me. Boy, did it feel good. After a bit, I leaned over and let the spray massage my head and neck. After a while, I turned around and let the water pelt my shoulder muscles. It irritated Daddy for me to take a long shower, but I didn't care. Turning first one way and then another, I showered until there was no more hot water.

A few minutes later, I was dressed in some of the clothes Lucille and Susie had pulled down to the right end of my closet. With the weight I had lost, I didn't own much that I could still wear. Without my belt, I literally couldn't keep most of my pants up.

Like always, Daddy had moved fast, and as I was putting my feet into my loafers, he started calling for me to meet him at the front door. I eased off my bed and reached out my hand to touch the walls so I could guide myself. Moving slowly and touching familiar things as I advanced, I made my way to where Daddy was. He held the door open for me, and I was doing OK until I misjudged where the threshold was and stumbled as I stepped over it.

With an uncharacteristic softness in his voice, Daddy said, "Be careful, Buddy. You might hurt yourself."

Not so softly in return I said, "I'm doing the best I can." I hated being so damn helpless, and if someone was even mildly critical of what I did I would usually get mad, and I didn't bother to try to hide it.

The distance from the front door of the house to the carport was only about fifteen feet, but walking even that short a distance was something of a strain. A few minutes after we pulled out of our driveway and turned right on Terry Road, I fell asleep.

The next thing I knew, Daddy called my name to wake me up. By the time I had my head clear enough to remember what I was doing, he had my car door open. I stepped out and reached for his right arm. As long as I was holding on to him, I could keep my balance easily, and I didn't have to worry about running into anything. I did fine up to the building that housed Dr. Hughes office, and as we got close to it some nice person spoke to us and held the door open. Invariably courteous, Daddy thanked him for his kindness.

When Dr. Hughes examined me a little while later, I could hear him turning something on and off as he got down close to my eye, but I couldn't see anything he was doing. After a little bit, he said he wasn't sure what had happened but that my inability to see could be caused by a blood clot blocking out the light. He prescribed some medicine for me to take and then suggested I might consult another ophthalmologist named Sam Johnson for a second opinion. As we left Daddy thanked Dr. Hughes for all the help he had been.

When we got in the car, Daddy talked about how nice Dr. Hughes was and how badly he had wanted me to be able to see. I, too, was impressed with the kindness of Dr. Hughes, but his recommendation that I see another ophthalmologist did nothing to allay my fears. In fact his recommendation made them worse.

The week between my visit with Dr. Hughes and my scheduled visit with Dr. Sam Johnson was the longest week of my life. Nothing I did or thought gave me any significant relief. I couldn't sleep well, and I found myself being unkind to everybody who came my way. I knew I was being awful, but I couldn't seem to stop myself. Maybe in my despair, I thought somehow I could feel better if I made others feel worse. I didn't achieve the first objective, but I surely did achieve the second one.

When my appointment with Dr. Johnson finally came, I got a more thorough examination than that given by Dr. Hughes, but the results were still not conclusive. Dr. Johnson wasn't sure what the final outcome was going to be for my eye, but I could tell he thought things didn't look good.

Before Daddy and I left his office, Dr. Johnson offered us a suggestion about how Daddy could serve as my guide. He said if I would hold my arms out like the tongue of a wagon, it would be easy to turn me right or left as needed. Daddy thanked him as he took my left hand and touched it against his right arm.

Walking back toward our car, I had the same worried feeling that I'd been having, but I also thought about Dr. Johnson's suggestion. I created a mental image of what Daddy and I would look like as he pulled me along. Damn, I thought, that's the dumbest idea I ever heard. It was also puzzling to think that a man smart enough to become an ophthalmologist would make such a recommendation.

In the days following my visit with Dr. Johnson, more and more of my blood clots began to dissolve. As this happened, however, no vision was returning. It was as if a light had been turned off and there was no way to turn it back on.

In desperation, we decided to go to Ochsner's Clinic in New Orleans for further consultation. Everyone knew of the great work they were doing in various fields, and we figured if anybody would know what to do for me, the experts at Ochsner's would.

Linda Jean was staying at Daddy's to be with me during that time, and on the appointed day, she, my brother-in-law Bill, Daddy, and I drove down to New Orleans together. Bill not only helped with the driving, he also gave some additional moral support – something all of us needed very badly.

When my eye was examined at Ochsner's, we all knew that whatever I was told would likely be the final outcome. The head of the clinic was working with me and there was no mistaking his level of expertise.

Following an exhaustive inspection of my eye, Dr. Ochsner told all of us his findings. He said that my retina had become completely detached and that, quite obviously, such an injury was very serious. He went on to say that though there was a physician in California who could reattach retinas, he would not be able to help me because mine had folded up. I didn't claim to know much about retinas, but even I could tell that there probably wasn't much hope for mine.

Thank goodness, I had people with me who loved me when I learned how bad things really were. Down deep, I suspected no one was surprised, but that didn't stop the hurt. Dr. Ochsner had shown deep human compassion when he gave us the bad news, and we all appreciated him having done that, but his predicted outcome made a feeling of hopelessness descend on me.

On our way back, Linda Jean let me put my head in her lap. I kept it there the entire trip and withdrew into myself. For the next four hours, I struggled without much success to find answers to all the questions that kept repeating themselves in my head.

Perhaps I should have accepted Dr. Ochsner's conclusions as being the final word, but I just couldn't do it. As a result, when I heard about a physician in Memphis, named McKinney, only a few days after I got back from New Orleans, I decided I had to go see him.

Daddy agreed with me, and we made an appointment for the following week. Because of the convenience of it, we decided to go by train. As it happened, my girlfriend was able to take off, so the three of us made our plans to go together.

Since my appointment in Memphis was going to give me my first opportunity to ride on a train, if circumstances had been different, I would have been excited. Regretfully, other emotions predominated.

From the beginning of the trip until we were on the outskirts of Memphis, I was anxious and fretful. No doubt I would have stayed that way for the entire time except for an incident with Daddy that had the effect of providing me with some much needed comic relief. The incident that enabled me to get a good chuckle involved the use of a pint-sized bathroom compartment. Having never been on a train before, the use of its facilities presented a unique experience that caused me more than a little apprehension. Daddy apparently saw the uncertainty registering on my face as I stood in front of a very small commode and tried to get myself centered. Acting decisively, he stepped up behind me and surveyed the situation, carefully assessing my state of readiness, as it were. Presumably, he found everything to be as it should be because he said, "Okay, Buddy, shoot!"

Daddy could be funny when he wanted to, and I knew that was one of those occasions so I decided to go along with him and get a laugh out of my discomfort. Prudently, however, I held back until I had finished that for which I had come. Then, and only then, did I let myself have the good laugh that I wanted, and in light of what was going to soon happen, what I would wind up needing.

As I had feared, something occurred in a little while that evoked an emotion so far from laughter the two shouldn't even be considered as being on the same spectrum. After my final ophthalmological expert, Dr. McKinney, finished his examination, he spoke to me in such a blunt manner, I was appalled at his demeanor. What he said was plenty bad enough, but the way he said it made it even worse. Without any preliminaries and without the tone of compassion used by Dr. Ochsner, he said, "Son, you're blind, and that's all there is to it. There's nothing I or anybody else can do for you. Your eye is damaged beyond repair. You might as well get accustomed to listening to the radio because you won't be watching any TV."

I had tried to prepare myself for that type of outcome, but I couldn't have anticipated the way I was to learn what I didn't want to know. Feeling stunned but scared and sad, I called Daddy and my girlfriend to my side. Holding each by the hand, I dropped my head and let the tears flow. I didn't cry long, though. Perhaps I was mad enough at Dr. McKinney to want to deny him the experience of seeing me giving the appearance of being defeated. With more confidence in my voice than was in my soul, I stood and said, "Let's go home."

On the way back, my girlfriend shared with me her determination to improve her ability to describe things to me. I thought that was sweet and sensitive, but I also detected what was at first an indefinable tone to her voice. After a moment, though, I was able to identify it. It was the tone of pity. From that moment our future was sealed. We continued our relationship for several more months, but that only served to assure our mutual unhappiness.

With his usual single-minded determination, Daddy got Bill to line me up with Mississippi's Rehabilitation for the Blind almost as soon as we got back to Jackson. Within days, I was visited by a rehab counselor who brought me a talking book player and a cane only three and a half feet long. With embarrassment, he explained that the cane was too short for me, but it was the longest one currently available. Then, despite his admission that the cane wasn't appropriate for me, he insisted on showing me how it might be put to use.

Perhaps it was his ridiculously ineffective instructions about how I could use a cane to get around that turned me against him. Or maybe, I just didn't like his cocksure personality. At any rate, after a brief visit with him, I was ready to go back to my room and pull out my hair.

As usual, Daddy was more tolerant and patient than I, and he found several reasons for me to continue my relationship with him. Among other things, Daddy figured I would enjoy the talking books, and he turned out to be more correct on that count than he could possibly imagine. It was also his belief we needed help in figuring out something I might do to make a living. Obviously, that was a goal that had to be reached above all others. The idea that I might be reduced to being a recipient of public assistance was unacceptable.

The Heidelberg Hotel had a nice gift shop that presumably provided a living for the person who ran it. It was Daddy's idea that I might be able to do something like that. I wasn't necessarily opposed to doing that kind of work, but I was at a loss about how I could manage any kind of job. Everything seemed to require vision, and I hated the prospect of having to contend with life unable to see something even right in front of my nose.

My rehabilitation counselor came back to see me a few days after his initial visit, and on that occasion, he talked about the importance of me learning some skills I would need by attending a rehabilitation center. That idea had no appeal for me whatever, and I told him so. I could have gone on to say that, in fact, the word rehabilitation was offensive to me. It wouldn't have mattered though because he was only listening to himself.

I soon learned that Daddy and I were in complete disagreement with respect to my counselor and what he proposed. Not only did Daddy fail to see how stupid the man was, he actually thought his ideas made a great deal of sense. Perhaps other family members were in agreement with Daddy, but I didn't give them much of a chance to influence me. I didn't want to go to a damn rehabilitation center and be forced to associate with a bunch of blind people, and that's all there was to it.

During the following several days, I spent most of my time in bed as I had been doing for months, but I did occupy some of my waking hours with meaningful activity. A lovely lady named Bobbie Austin who was a next door neighbor, came by regularly and read articles to me from various periodicals. As usual, Maureen and I talked every day by phone, and friends were still stopping by, although somewhat less frequently.

I wasn't well yet. In fact, I was still weak, but I had gained a few pounds and was no longer sleeping fifteen hours or more per day. Daddy interpreted these changes to mean it was time for me to get up and get out. He made his case to me one day following yet another unwanted visit from my rehab counselor. Once more, the counselor had made me as mad as hell by bringing up the idea of a rehabilitation center, but that time he mentioned one by name. He told me he thought Arkansas Enterprises for the Blind in Little Rock would be a good place for me because it specialized in helping adults to adjust to being blind.

My counselor had left fairly soon after I had thrown my cane down and told him a thing or two. I wouldn't say that he left in a huff, but I would say that when he departed he didn't say much about a return visit.

Daddy witnessed my behavior with the counselor and, perhaps, that even strengthened his conviction as to what was best for me. At any rate, Daddy told me once again of his firm belief that I needed to get some help. We argued heatedly, and I told him that he was meddling with my damn business. He gave me to understand that it wasn't just my business and that I needed to be more mature in my thinking.

The longer we talked, the more heated our arguments became. We both vented our feelings freely and a lot of what each of us said was to be firmly implanted in my memory. More clearly than anything else, I remember Daddy's last words on the subject of me attending the rehabilitation center in Little Rock, Arkansas. He said, "Hell yes, you are going, too."

Chapter 5

Learning to Live Without Light

Once the decision had been made that I was going to attend the rehabilitation center, things moved very quickly. In a matter of days, Daddy and I were on our way to Little Rock, Arkansas. Since our route took us through Vicksburg, it was convenient for us to pick up our friend Jim Simmons so he could accompany us and help Daddy with the driving. Mr. Jim had been a great friend since my accident, visiting often and bringing me little gifts. His enjoyment of life was infectious, and his company was especially helpful as I was being taken to a place where I did not want to be.

We were riding in Daddy's black Packard Clipper, a sleek-looking car with a supercharged engine. If you weren't careful, you would be driving a great deal faster than you intended. That point was made very clear halfway into our trip when Mr. Jim, who had taken the wheel in Vicksburg, happened to look at the speedometer and declared that he better slow down. We had been driving along at ninety miles per hour on a highway where the speed limit was never more than sixty.

I sat on the backseat so I could stretch out my leg. Though my knee was completely healed, my leg always felt better when it wasn't bent. My calf still wasn't well, but it was much better than it had been. Either the staph infection was gone from my body for a time or it had shifted to another place.

Even though the trip only took us about six hours, I spent a good bit of time sleeping. Daddy and Mr. Jim talked quite a bit, but Daddy caught a nap or two as well.

We got to the rehabilitation center in mid afternoon and met a few of the staff members. One of them, Mrs. Plant, showed me to a room on the second floor of the building that housed several offices and the dining hall. After giving me a very brief orientation to the room with its adjoining bath, she went back to other duties, leaving Daddy, Mr. Jim, and me to say our good byes. Since their drive back lay before them, our farewells had to be quick. It was a good thing too. Daddy wasn't good at controlling his emotions and, as I quickly learned, Mr. Jim was no better. The two of them cried as they held me in their arms for a moment or two. I could feel Daddy's body shaking as he sobbed his good bye, and I had a hard time letting him go. I was shaking with my own sobs and having him to hold onto helped me.

When they left, I fumbled my way over to the bed I had been assigned and lay down. The turmoil of the entire experience had worn me out. I was stronger than I had been when I left the hospital, but I was a world away from being robust. Fully clothed, I weighed 113 pounds. Assuming my cast had weighed about two pounds; that meant I had gained seven pounds in the six months since my accident.

Mrs. Plant had told me supper would be served about 5:30, which I knew would be coming pretty soon, but I couldn't look forward to it. In fact, as I lay there, I dreaded the prospect of going down to the dining hall. The truth was, I didn't have the vaguest idea of how to get there. I was completely disoriented and the cane that had been given to me by my rehab counselor was of virtually no use. God, I thought, what on earth is going to happen to me?

Fortunately, I didn't have very long to feel miserable in that strange place all by myself because only a few minutes after Daddy and Mr. Jim left, I heard several other people talking not very far away. One of them, a lady with a pleasant voice but a strange sounding accent, came over and spoke to me. She introduced herself as Mrs. Clifford from Columbia City, Indiana. She said she and her husband had just brought their son Frankie down to the center and that I'd meet him later. Talking nonstop, she went on to say she hoped we'd be friends and then asked if I'd like to pet her little dog. Actually, I didn't want to, but that didn't seem to occur to her as she put him on my chest and explained he was a Chihuahua who loved people. Knowing what I was expected to do, I pretended to be pleased as I patted his funny-feeling little head.

A moment later there was the sound of other people coming into the room. As I suspected, it was her husband and son, and after they finished putting things away, she called them over and introduced all of us. They had the same kind of accent that she did, and although I found it unusual, I didn't find it unpleasant.

It was very clear that Mrs. Clifford did virtually all the talking in their little family. Both Mr. Clifford and Frankie said they were pleased to meet me, but after that, they didn't seem to have anything else to add.

Soon Mrs. Clifford herded them outside the room so she and Mr. Clifford could tell Frankie good bye. I heard every word they said to one another, and it was obvious Frankie's parents hated to leave their son as badly as Daddy had hated to leave me.

After his parents had gone, Frankie came back into our room and started putting his clothes away. He talked a little as he worked but not very much. It didn't appear that he and I were going to have much in common, since he, obviously, was the quiet type.

A little while later, several other people came in. They all introduced themselves to Frankie and me, since we were the new kids on the block. One of them was an older guy from Oklahoma, named Bob Spain. Two others were young fellows from New Mexico and Arizona – Conrad Young and Wilson Nelson. Very quickly, I learned about each of them. For example, I learned that Conrad, like me, had only been blind for a very short time, but, unlike me, his blindness was the result of a brain tumor. I found him to be an especially nice person, and I think he and I could have been great friends, but as I was soon to discover, a brain tumor doesn't give you much of a chance. Within a few months, he was dead.

Bob Spain, like Frankie, was blind because of Diabetes. Both of them had some useful sight, but little by little, what they had was being lost. It didn't take me long to understand that Diabetes, like a brain tumor, can also take a terrible toll.

Wilson Nelson was different from all the rest of us in that he had been blind virtually all his life. Something had injured his eyes when he was a baby and he had no memory of ever seeing. He was different from the rest of us in another way, too. Rather than being descended from European ancestry, he was a full-blooded Navajo Indian.

In a little while, they helped me get down to the dining hall, where I not only had a nice meal, but also an opportunity to meet a number of females who were in training. Being around anyone who was blind was a new experience for me, but being in the company of girls who were blind made the experience even more unusual. For a while, I found it somehow disconcerting.

After supper was over, I joined several other trainees in the parlor just outside the dining hall where we sat and talked for a few minutes. Mostly, I just listened and tried to figure out who each speaker was. I felt on edge because I wasn't having much success. I hoped my confusion was the result of my fatigue, but I was pretty sure it wasn't. Identifying people by their voice was going to be a real challenge.

To my immense relief, one of the fellows from my room said he was going upstairs and asked if I would like to come along. "Thanks," I said in his general direction, as I stood and almost lost my balance. Fortunately, he had walked over to me, and as I bumped against him, I was able to right myself. As if nothing had happened, he suggested I take his left arm and let him guide me back to our room. After a little fumbling, I found his arm and held onto it until we made it back to our room. I wasn't sure who my guide was and was too embarrassed to ask, but as we walked together, I had what undoubtedly would have appeared to be a sardonic smile on my face because I was thinking of some words from the New Testament. "If the blind lead the blind, they will fall into a ditch."

Once my guide had directed me to my bed, I felt a little more relaxed. Although I couldn't visualize how things were laid out, I knew for sure the bathroom was right by my bed. That knowledge gave me enough feeling of security to prevent all the other uncertainties from overwhelming me. Even so, it was close.

Sheer exhaustion caused me to sleep, and I awakened the next morning to the noises of my roommates getting ready to go down for breakfast. I struggled out of bed and made my way to the bathroom. Both lavatories seemed to be occupied, but that did not matter to me. I was seeking another fixture, and thank goodness, I found it in time. A moment later, I also found a vacant lavatory, but in the process, I bumped into one of my roommates. "Sorry," I said. "Don't worry about it," he said, whoever he was. When I got back to my bed, after washing my hands, I decided I'd better go ahead and take a shower rather than risk not having enough time to do it later. Then, to my disgust, I found I was scared to try. Everything was so strange to me; I had to force myself to do much of anything.

After sitting on my bed and feeling sorry for myself a while, I finally found enough courage to get up and give it a try. Acting before my courage could leave me, I got up and stripped. Making my way to a shower stall turned out to be easy, but I knew, once I was inside, I'd still have the problem of finding the soap. Since the stall was quite small, I didn't see how that would be much of a challenge, and I was only a little wrong. Once I had the faucets located, I felt first to the right and then to the left, but to my dismay my hand touched only a blank wall. Finally, thank goodness, I found it. The problem, I discovered, was that the soap dish was considerably higher than I had expected.

A few moments later I made it back to my bed. I was clean, and for a moment, felt some satisfaction about what I'd been able to do, but that was quickly followed by a feeling of dread. I had just realized I couldn't remember how to get to my chest of drawers. Blithely unaware of my distress, my roommates were talking with one another and even laughing together as they engaged in their various activities, whatever the hell they were.

Rather than admit my confusion and ask someone for help, I sat down on my bed and tried to clear my head. With everything going on around me and the noises I was hearing somewhere outside our room, it wasn't easy to do. I had the kind of feeling I would get when I was losing my balance. Regardless of how I held my head, I couldn't gain the feeling of normal equilibrium. Hoping a complete change in my posture would help, I lay down on my bed.

Putting my hands up to my ears to block out some of the noise, I started trying to recall what Mrs. Plant had told me before about the location of my chest of drawers. As the moments passed and I adjusted to being in a prone position, something approaching relaxation began to occur. Gradually, I got enough under control to think clearly, and I could hear Mrs. Plant's voice in my head as she told me about my bed and where the bathroom was and then, hallelujah, that my chest of drawers was four feet down the wall from the foot of my bed.

With a feeling of relief, mixed with a measure of satisfaction, I rolled out of bed and went directly where I intended. I opened first the top drawer and then the second. I selected the clothes I needed and went back to my bed. I was soon dressed in a pair of jeans with a pullover shirt and ready for whatever the day might hold. At least from the standpoint of looking presentable, I hoped.

Clutching the cane Mrs. Plant had given me, I sat on my bed and waited for someone to help me get downstairs to the dining hall. As I listened to the various sounds about me, I became aware that things were not nearly as noisy as they had been. That made me wonder if I was going to be left to fend for myself, and I began to feel my stomach muscles tighten. Not being willing to prolong my agony, I asked the space in front of me if any could help me get downstairs. To my immense relief, I heard a short laugh, followed by, "What's the matter, Mississippi, are you getting hungry?" Hoping I hadn't sounded too pathetic and also thinking I should buck up a little, I replied, "As a matter of fact, I am. I was just thinking how good a plate of grits and eggs would taste with, maybe, a little piece of ham and redeye gravy." The laughter occurred again and then the fellow said, "Well, fall in behind me, and we'll go down and see what's available. If I were you, I wouldn't count on the redeye gravy. Now that I think about it, I wouldn't count on the grits either." As the man talked, I heard him walking toward me with an occasional tapping sound made by his cane and then, for a moment, he was right in front of me. After taking a few additional steps, he stopped and asked if I was with him. "I am now," I said as I moved toward his voice. "I'll keep talking as we walk, so you can easily tell where I am. By the way, Jimmy, in case you haven't recognized me yet, my name is Bob Spain. You may recall I'm the older guy in the group, and I'm from Oklahoma." I was about to respond when Bob said, "Hold it right here now, we've come to the gate at the head of the stairs. Step up here behind me if you want to and put your hand on it so you can see how it works."

I did as he suggested and noted that it only swung inward, which of course, made good sense. That way it served as a barrier to the stairs and was an easy means of preventing an accident. "Thanks," I said as I let the gate close and stepped back.

"Let me go first since I'm familiar with things," Bob said, and in a moment I heard the gate open and close. "Come on now," Bob said, "and be sure and hold onto the rail as we descend. It would be bad for my reputation if I let you fall."

I did as he suggested, and noticed again that my right leg was doing OK but still too stiff to permit me to descend the stairs quickly. Each time I had to step down on my right foot and then bring the left one down beside it.

In a moment, Bob announced he was on the landing and would be turning right to reach the second flight. Soon I reached it too, and held firmly to the rail as I continued to follow my new friend.

As soon as we entered the dining hall, a young woman came up and offered me her arm, telling me her name was Juanita and that she would show me to my table after we picked up my food. I could tell by her voice that she was a pleasant person, but something about the way she sounded made me wonder if she was black. Then as she guided over to pick up my food and to my table, I thought, now isn't this interesting. This woman, who may or may not be a Negro, is helping me. Do I care one way or the other? I asked myself. After a moment's reflection, I knew the answer. I didn't care, not one iota.

As Juanita sat my plate on the table, she took my right hand and placed it on the back of a chair while at the same introducing me to my tablemate, Judy. After Judy and I spoke to one another, Juanita broke in to tell me she'd come back after I had finished eating and give me further assistance. Judy and I chatted some as we ate, but I mostly concentrated on finding my food and trying to be sure I didn't spill my milk.

True to her word, Juanita came over as I was finishing breakfast and gave me a little additional orientation. She explained to me that soon I would be expected to pick up my own plate and return it after I had finished eating. Steadily talking as she cleared the table, she offered me her right arm and showed me how to get back to the serving area. Continuing to talk in a comfortable and straightforward manner as we walked upstairs to my room, she said I'd have a few minutes to do whatever I needed to do before Mrs. Plant would come back and begin to show me around. Soon I had the room and bathroom to myself. Bob Spain and Frank Clifford were the only two guys left when Juanita showed me to my bed and, very shortly, both of them departed.

Concerned, as always, about my teeth, I went to the bathroom and gave them a good scrubbing. It was a good thing I did, too, because as soon as I walked out of the bathroom, Mrs. Plant announced her arrival.

Like the day before, I found her to be pleasant and upbeat, and, as I was discovering, a good talker. She didn't skip a beat from the moment we left my room until she had me properly introduced to Miss Lila Lampkin, secretary to Mr. Roy Kumpe, who was head of the entire center. Miss Lampkin and I got off to a great start, largely because she was very nice to me and very complimentary of Mississippi.

Following our brief chat, Miss Lampkin directed me back to Mr. Kumpe's office and introduced the two of us. I stuck out my hand in what I thought was the right direction, but he did not grasp it. Then, seconds later, his hand grasped mine, and he pumped it up and down vigorously as he told me how delighted he was to meet me. From the tone of his voice I knew he was sincere, and I quickly warmed up to him.

He told me all about the center and how, with the support of the Lions Club, it has been helping adults adjust to blindness ever since 1947. Other historical details didn't stick with me, but they seemed to be important to him so I tried to act interested. He touched on the current activities of the center, too, and what I would be doing. It was easy for me to listen, but I was still having trouble keeping things straight. My nose was stopped up, and my mouth seemed to be getting drier by the second. I also had an uncomfortable feeling in my chest, a kind of tightness that contributed to my discomfort. Some of what Mr. Kumpe was saying began to bother me, too. It didn't look like he could say two sentences without using the word "blind." I was getting tired of hearing it and ready to move on to something else. There must not have been anything else, though, because all the way up to the end of our session, that seemed to be all we talked about.

Eventually, we must have reached a stopping point because Mr. Kumpe asked me if I had any final questions for him. Feeling some relief, I told him that I didn't. "OK," he said as he came around to my side of the desk and offered me his left arm. "Let's go see our psychologist, Mr. Thume." He apparently heard us coming because, even before Mr. Kumpe introduced us, he was calling me by name and offering me a chair. Mr. Kumpe must have taken that as his cue to depart. He laid my hand on the back of the chair, said good morning to Mr. Thume and good bye to me.

Mr. Thume was much more soft-spoken than Mr. Kumpe and much less outgoing, it seemed, but I figured maybe psychologists were like that. I had no grounds for such a judgment, having only heard of psychologists before, but like most people, I supposed, I had my ideas.

No doubt Mr. Thume asked me various questions during our first conversation, but details did not remain with me. My general impression did, however, and it was one of a man who was understanding and could be relied upon to be helpful in any way he could.

After the midmorning coffee break, in which all staff and trainees participated, I met the man who was in charge of cane travel. His name was Oliver Burke and it was he who would be primarily responsible for teaching me how to walk safely and independently with the aid of a cane. He substituted a longer cane for the one Mrs. Plant had given me the day before and then proceeded to give me rudimentary instructions on how to use it. After spending only a few minutes inside, he guided me to a sidewalk where, he explained in more detail how the cane had to be used. It sounded simple enough. All I had to do was touch the cane down at the place where I would plant my foot each time I took a step. That meant, of course, the cane had to be swung from side to side in perfect rhythm with my walking pattern. Mr. Burke explained it would take a while to learn how to do that well. Boy, was he right.

A little before eleven, Mr. Burke showed me to the meeting room for what, he explained, was an eleven o'clock discussion session. By then I had learned enough to suit me about cane travel and was plenty ready to sit down. Directing me to a chair, Mr. Burke indicated that all the trainees would be there and I would also have the opportunity to meet Bunk Goodrum, the staff member who would lead the discussion that day. What an interesting name, I thought, as I gratefully sat down and stretched out my legs.

The session was called to order, and the person doing the talking identified himself as Bunk Goodrum, for the benefit of the new trainees, as he explained. I learned later that he did quite a bit of the public relations work for the center, but right then what I learned was that he was good at conducting a meeting. As he spoke, we were all quiet and, as far as I could tell, attentive. The first order of business, as he explained, would be to present two new trainees, one from Indiana named Frank Clifford and one from Mississippi named Jimmy Robertson.

After giving Frank and me a brief welcome, he asked all the other trainees to stand and introduce themselves one by one beginning on his left. Dutifully, the introductions began, and each trainee shared a little information about background and interests. One trainee, a fellow named Steve, who, like Frankie was from Indiana, made the group laugh by telling all the girls that he wasn't married.

Following their introductions, Bunk asked me to stand and share a few things with the group. Knowing my turn would be coming, I had already prepared my opening remarks. The fellow Steve had given me a perfect entrée, and I took advantage of it. I said, "As you heard, I'm Jimmy Robertson from Liberty, Mississippi, and I want you to know, I'm not married either. Steve said he wasn't married, but he didn't give you any of his qualifications." As I had hoped, that comment brought substantial laughter from the group.

When it died down, with what turned out to be perfect timing, I said, "I want you girls to know that I am extremely good looking." Again, as I had hoped, I got a good response. Feeling fortified, I continued to talk, purely for their entertainment. I gave them a little foolishness about what a great personality I had, how I had a substantial amount of money, and various other qualifications that made me a great catch. When I finished, with them still laughing, I got a nice little round of applause.

Bunk had obviously enjoyed my remarks, too, because with laughter in his voice, he said, "Jimmy, it sounds as if you found yourself an avocation." I had heard that term before, and as I thought about it for a moment, I suspected Bunk might be correct. I surely hoped he was. For as many years as I could remember, giving people a reason to laugh was what I enjoyed above virtually anything. If I could continue to do that, I knew in my heart of hearts it would serve me well.

During the remainder of that day, I met my other teachers and discovered a little about what each of them would be helping me learn. I would have Mrs. Lorene Gibson for Braille, Mr. Robert King for shop and woodworking, Mrs. Rena Mae Metcalf for crafts, and Mrs. Betty Jean Goodrum, Bunk's wife, for daily demands of living. Normally, I would have each class for a 45-minute period every day.

It was obvious that the most important skill I needed to gain was that of cane travel. If I could walk independently and go where I wanted and needed to go, many other things would fall into place. I didn't minimize the importance of the other skills I would hopefully be acquiring, but I would be spending more time with Mr. Burke than anyone. What I didn't know was exactly how true that was. By the time I finally finished my training, I had experienced both excruciating frustration and finally, remarkable achievement.

When my first full day's activities concluded at 4:30, I was exhausted. Fortunately, there was a short period before dinnertime, during which I could rest. I flopped down on my bed and immediately felt drowsy. The attic fan created enough of a breeze to make the old Brack Mansion comfortable, and if my roommates hadn't been making so much noise, I would have fallen asleep. Well, I thought, if I can't do that, at least I can rest a little.

In a little while, Bob Spain asked if I wanted his help to get down the stairs. Feeling very grateful for his offer, I told him I did. For the life of me I couldn't figure out where I was in the building and how to get down to the dining hall. Just thinking about all that made my head hurt.

That night after supper, I sat around and visited in the parlor for quite a little while with the other trainees who lingered there. A couple of them seemed a little slow, almost childlike, but the others appeared quite normal. I listened to their conversations and joined in occasionally when given an opportunity. The fact that they all knew each other put me at a disadvantage, but I tried to not let that bother me. What I couldn't keep from bothering me, however, was my fatigue. Fairly soon, I asked my friend, Bob Spain, to help me get back upstairs, so I could go to bed.

What I learned the next and in succeeding days of my training was that I was quite good at mastering or refining some skills but barely adequate at others. In the instance of Braille, for example, I quickly memorized most of the symbols necessary for reading and writing, but the sense of touch and manual dexterity required that I do them quickly were other matters entirely. Since everything in Braille involves one or more of the six dots that form a full Braille cell, much like the dots on a domino, memorizing the fundamentals was easy. Very soon, I could tell you that dot one was the letter "A," dots one and two make the letter "B," one and four, the letter "C," etc. What I couldn't do quickly, however, was feel the dots and read the words they formed. Nor could I write the letters quickly using a slate and stylus. I marveled at my fellow trainees who had known Braille all of their lives and could read and write it virtually as fast as I read and wrote the printed word as a sighted person. I suspected I would never be fluent in Braille, but I figured I had better learn enough to at least get by, and as it turned out, that was exactly what I did.

I found that Mrs. Betty Goodrum's Daily Demands of Living class was important to me because, as suggested by the title, I was learning skills every person would need to have. Mrs. Goodrum was a fine teacher, too. Under her patient tutelage, I sharpened my typing and other communication skills and learned enough about cooking to manage the preparation of a simple meal. Those accomplishments were important unto themselves, but their ultimate impact had very broad implications. As I crossed the great chasm between helplessness and the ability to accomplish the myriad tasks necessary for independent living, I was gaining the conviction that virtually nothing of importance would be impossible for me to master.

If I had experienced the same level of success in my efforts to master cane travel, my life would have been a whole lot simpler. But that wasn't the way it was – not for quite a while. As the summer wore on, I continued to practice my cane techniques, but I couldn't get the rhythm right. As a result, I couldn't keep myself from making mistakes, such as accidentally stepping off the sidewalk or even a curb, occasionally. My greatest problem, however, lay in the fact that I was unable to walk in anything like a straight line from point A to point B. As a result, crossing a wide driveway or street without anything other than my sense of direction to use as a guide was an unbelievable challenge. Time after time I would wind up where I didn't intend to be and often would be as lost as a goose. Mr. Burke worked with me patiently on the grounds of the center and even out into the neighborhood, but I couldn't reach the point where I felt in control. On the contrary, I consistently felt as if my equilibrium had been lost along with my eyesight. Having never had a great sense of direction, without my eyes to find some guideposts, I was virtually always confused about where I was.

My fellow trainees knew I was having a difficult time in this most important area of my rehabilitation, and several of them tried to be helpful. They gave me such pointers as the need to listen for auditory cues that would help to provide a sense of direction. I tried hard to use these suggestions, but often I found the noises about me actually added to my confusion and, sometimes, to my fear as well. If, for example, I was walking down a sidewalk alongside a street and a car passed, rather than its sound being of any help to me, I would often think that I was in danger of being run over.

One day in late July, I reached the breaking point. I had followed all of the instructions Mr. Burke had given me and used the advice provided by my fellow trainees who got around without apparent difficulty, but I had achieved nothing remotely comparable to competence. After accidentally stepping off a familiar sidewalk for the fifteenth time, I threw my cane down and cursed it for the useless son-of-a-bitch that it was. I was never going to learn how to use it, and I knew it. In fact, I declared that to be the case in a loud voice and my choice of words would have sent my Sunday school teacher into apoplexy. For a long time, I just stood there and felt helpless. It was the worst day I had experienced at the center and, for that matter, one of the worst days of my life. I knew I had to overcome the problems I was having in getting about, but I just couldn't do it. Oh, was I miserable. Finally, though still feeling utterly defeated, I picked up my cane and resumed my efforts. As I feared, in a moment I stepped off the sidewalk once again. Lord, I thought, what in the world am I going to do?

Since at any given time there were only about fifteen of us in training at the center, we got to know one another fairly well. Inevitably, I compared myself to the fellows who were about my age, and, to my dismay, virtually all of them were doing better than I in cane travel. They were aware of this fact, and a couple of them tried to help me individually but to no real avail.

Fortunately, there was an older trainee named Tom Douglas who decided to take me on as a personal project. Despite his relatively advanced years and serious physical problems associated with Diabetes, he was learning to get about quite well, and he was mystified by my lack of success. He was a big talker and, to be frank, quite full of himself, but since he was trying to be helpful to me, I did nothing to discourage him.

One afternoon when our classes were over, he decided to take things in hand. At his suggestion, we walked out to the front of the training building, Old Barry Hall, and he began to give me little assignments. To our mutual dismay, I didn't do very well with them because of my old problem of not being able to walk in a straight line. Acting as if he was Mr. Burke, Tom asked me several questions about what I was doing and not doing. Then, as if he had become inspired, he asked me to show him how I was holding my cane. I did so, and he immediately recommended a change. He suggested I extend both my index finger and my thumb along the side of the cane. I had not thought of this as an alternative because wrapping all four fingers and my thumb around the cane had seemed comfortable to me. With nothing to lose, however, I changed my grip and gave it a try. I saw an almost instant improvement. The new grip was more comfortable and it afforded me greater control. Tom had not given me a silver bullet, but he had definitely helped me, and I told him so. He fairly preened for several days after that.

My progress in learning to get around well continued to be slower than I would have liked, but things were getting somewhat better. I continued to grip my cane the way Tom had suggested, and that was serving me well, but I could also tell a difference in my physical wellbeing. Although my weight had increased very little since being at the center, my muscle tone was improving and that was also serving me quite well. By mid-August, it began to appear I might even be ready to try for the goal of earning a solo pin. The very name of that pin testified to its importance, and not all trainees could hope to earn it. Doing so required skill, stamina, and self confidence. The distance covered by the solo route was at least one mile. Mr. Burke would walk it with you, pointing out potential problems as he did, but on the day of your attempt, it was all up to you.

On a Tuesday in early September, my day finally came. During my bus ride from the center to Sixth and Main, my heart was beating faster than usual. As I stepped off of the bus, and began my route, my heart rate soared. I told myself over and over that I knew how to get to my destination at Broadway and Markham, but the prospect of crossing all those streets and remembering where I was and what I had yet to do was almost more than I could take.

Ignoring the traffic and all the other confusing noises as best I could, I walked up to the corner. As soon as I reached it, I asked a person on my left if I might get help crossing Main Street. Knowing you have to move very quickly when the light changes, I waited in vain for a response. Damn, I thought as people beside me stepped off the curb, and I collected my wits enough to follow them, this is going to be a long day. Knowing I couldn't dwell on that thought, however, I perked up my ears and tried to follow the sound of an unknown number of feet headed where I needed to go. Stumbling only slightly as I stepped up on the curb and turned north, I walked the few necessary feet to reach Sixth. Since it wasn't nearly as busy as Main, I decided to not even ask for assistance in crossing.

Knowing I had a straight shot and a wide sidewalk all the way up to Second, I relaxed a little. Being keyed up was making it hard for me to remember how many streets I had already crossed. Well I thought, just to be sure, when I come to the next street, I'll ask someone what it is. Having that reassurance will make things better, I thought, as the traffic noises signaled the next street I had to cross. To my dismay, however, when I found the curb and asked the name of the street, no one was there to hear my question. Fear welled up in me again as I waited and listened so I would know when to cross and, even more so, as I stepped off the curb and hoped I'd reach the other side where I needed to be.

Guiding myself quite satisfactorily by the traffic on my right, I crossed what I thought was Third and continued north on Main. In a moment, I heard people talking as they headed my way, and when I judged them to be at the right distance, I asked if the next street up was Second. "Of course, it is," a young girl said. "It's plainly marked." "Thank you," I replied as I resumed the rhythmical tapping of my cane and wondered if she had caught on.

At Second, I turned west and followed the sidewalk easily across both Louisiana and Center, but then I felt some apprehension because I couldn't remember if I would be crossing an alley between Center and Spring or Spring and Broadway. Well, I thought, I'll just check the next curb and see if there's a building right against it. If there was, I had found an alley. Sure enough, in a moment, that was exactly what happened. Smiling to myself, I made the short walk across it. I walked quickly up to Spring and, a few minutes later, had reached Broadway.

At Broadway, I crossed Second with ease, but I knew I'd have to have help in a few moments. Crossing Broadway and Markham by myself would be more of a risk than I was willing to take. I planned to stand and wait however long was necessary. Thankfully an old man came along in a moment, and I didn't even have to ask him for his help.

Once I was in front of City Hall, I climbed the two different sets of steps leading to the building and then simply followed the people noises to the door. Inside the building, I made my way over to the concession stand, run by a nice blind guy named Buddy, and ordered a Coke. He set it on the counter and held it until my hand touched it. After giving him my money, I lifted the bottle and took a big swallow. "Boy, was it good," I was thinking as he said, "That was a penny you gave me." "Oh Lord," I said, fumbling in my pocket for a nickel. "I wasn't trying to cheat you." "Of course, you weren't," he said with a chuckle. "You just made a mistake." I told him I was earning my solo pin and he congratulated me. "How long have you been blind?" he asked. "About seven months," I said, feeling tears well up in my eyes. "Looks like you're doing pretty well then," he said. "I guess so," I replied, but I couldn't muster much conviction. I was still worried about getting back to Main and down to Seventh without killing myself.

As I headed out a few moments later, a nice lady held the front door open for me and asked where I was going. When I told her, she said she'd be glad to assist me if I liked. "Yes'um," I said, reaching my left hand out for her right arm. "I would like that very much." Once we were across Markham and Broadway, I was on my own again, but the worst part was over. I picked up my pace and crossed Second a few moments later as if I had done it a hundred times. As I turned east, the tightness in my neck, which had begun the moment I stepped off the bus, began to subside. I knew I would easily recognize Main when I got to it, so I didn't bother to think about anything other than staying on the sidewalk and crossing the three streets and one alley between me and it. When I reached Main in what seemed like a very short period of time, I began to feel that my ordeal was essentially over. Counting the streets as I crossed them without even bothering to ask for assistance, I moved steadily toward Economy Drugstore at Seventh and Main. When I reached it, I must have been smiling from ear to ear because a man held the door open for me and said, "Here you go, Son." Mr. Burke came in a few minutes later and congratulated me. I thanked him and said I was glad it was over. Laughing, he replied, "Yes, but I have a lot more in mind for you." The next day at our 11:00 a.m. discussion meeting, Mr. Burke formally awarded me my solo pin. When the applause of my fellow trainees died down, he observed that the pin shows a cane with wings. What great symbolism, I thought, reaching for my handkerchief.

Earning a solo pin was my first major accomplishment at the center, but my success in my cane travel class was being duplicated in a number of other classes on a somewhat smaller scale. Generally speaking, I felt good about how I was doing, but one problem kept nagging at me, and I couldn't find a way to stop it. The thing that kept bothering me was the fact that although I was learning many things that I needed to know, I wasn't learning anything that would assure future employment. My friend, Bob Spain, who was about to complete his training, suggested that when my time was up I ought to come to Oklahoma so that the two of us could establish an insurance agency. I was flattered that he would think such a thing, but I had absolutely no interest in selling insurance. In fact, I could have made a very long list of things that I didn't want to do, or knew I couldn't do, but that was as far as I could go.

Though it bothered me to recall it, before my accident, I had spent very little time seriously considering what I might ultimately become. The very word, future, implied something so far away that I wouldn't need to be concerned about it until much later. The closest I had ever come to making any kind of a plan was the hope that someday I would be a college graduate. The truth was, though, I had no real strategy in mind to achieve that objective. No doubt, I had the general feeling that ultimately I'd work things out. My accident, however, changed all that.

What I knew for sure, after I became blind, was that coping with life day by day simply wasn't enough. The big picture was still out there somewhere, and I had to figure out how I was going to fit into it.

Though I could not have explained it, even after having been at the center for many weeks, what I needed was a meaningful role model. Many of my fellow trainees had shown me it was possible to become quite skilled in particular areas, but not a single one of them could be held up as a model for me to follow. I admired those who had musical ability, for example, but since I had no real interest in music and even less ability in that area, there was nothing for me to imitate. In many ways, of course, even those who had some special talent were in the same predicament as I. That fact became more and more obvious to me as my weeks in training began to pile up. Trainee after trainee would come to the end of his or her time at the center and be required to go back home. I often wondered if their lives would be dramatically different once they were back home. Obviously they were better off in many ways, but ultimately, what would that translate into? That's what I wanted to know, and that's what kept me continually on edge about my future.

Perhaps I would have eventually figured out on my own what I needed to do, but obviously there's no way to know that. As it happened, it didn't really matter because the problem was virtually taken out of my hands and my uncertainty was dispelled so quickly, I wondered later, with a smile, why I had worried so much about it in the first place. At the time it occurred though, what I experienced was relief followed fairly quickly by intense gratitude. Everything of importance related to my future would be directly related to that experience, and I knew it instantly. For me, it was an epiphany, but remarkably, it occurred almost casually.

One day about twelve weeks after my training had begun, Bunk Goodrum and I happened to run into one another in the parlor of the administration building. Since his responsibilities often took him away from the center, and I spent most of my time going to my various classes, he and I had not gotten to know one another very well at all. With both of us wanting to change that circumstance, we decided to sit down and visit.

Bunk complimented me on the progress he understood me to be making, and we talked a little about the difficulties inherent in adjusting to blindness. As conversations will do, ours moved quickly from one topic to another with no particular pattern emerging. Bunk asked me several questions, but they were of no great consequence. Then, out of the blue as it were, he asked me two questions that made all the difference in the world. First he asked me what I was going to do when I left the center. In complete honesty, I told him that I didn't have the vaguest idea. Pausing only a second after my response and then speaking in a manner that might suggest his next question was almost too obvious to be raised, he asked, "Why don't you go back to college?" His question was immediately followed by the simple declaration, "That's what I did." And I knew instantly I'd be doing what he had done.

Feeling as if a great burden had been lifted from my shoulders, I said, "Yes, I will. Yes. Yes." We talked for a little while after that, but it really wasn't necessary. I had learned what I needed to know. In fact, as Bunk went on to tell about some of his college experiences, I was barely listening. My attention had shifted from the present to the future, but this time when I thought about what was out there for me, I didn't feel so scared.

By the time I had my epiphany and also earned my solo pin, I had been at the center about three months. Throughout this period, I was taking all of the classes that were offered and each of them played a role in my total adjustment. Shop, handicrafts, and typing all improved my manual dexterity, which made countless other tasks easier. Similarly, as I learned to read and write Braille more fluently, I could make notes for myself and not have to rely exclusively on memory. For my cane travel classes, this would soon be essential because I could not commit to memory the many addresses I would be expected to locate.

What was happening was that a symbiotic relationship in all areas of my training was being established. Soon, the results of this relationship began to manifest themselves in a host of ways, and the pace of my adjustment began to escalate noticeably.

In the instance of cane travel for example, I was reaching the point where I could fairly easily take Mr. Burke's advanced assignments. They involved locating a number of downtown addresses without having previously been to any of them.

Many factors played a role in the quickening pace of my ability to go virtually anywhere I wished, but one of them took on a very different character from the others. It involved the development -- or perhaps the discovery-- of an ability known as obstacle perception. This is a phenomenon that refers to a blind person's ability to perceive the presence of various obstacles despite the fact they are not being seen. It could be compared to the feeling a sighted person would have when making a wrong turn in pitch darkness and sensing that he or she was about to walk into a corner.

Using this ability to any real advantage took quite a bit of time and effort, but eventually I found I could often put it to use. For instance, if I was walking down a sidewalk that was normally completely clear but on this occasion was not, because of an obstacle such as a car being parked across it, I would sense that a barrier lay in my path long before I had actually reached it. It wasn't completely reliable, of course, and occasionally I would believe I was perceiving a particular obstacle only to find that it was something else entirely. Once, for instance, when I approached a busy intersection in downtown Little Rock where I required assistance in order to cross the streets safely, I spoke to an obstacle I assumed to be a person but turned out to be a telephone pole. Until I discovered the mistake I'd made, I was pretty miffed at being ignored.

Another discovery I made insofar as my abilities were concerned was that I turned out to be somewhat brighter than I had assumed. Given my record throughout school and especially in college, there was no reason to believe I possessed anything other than normal intelligence, and perhaps below normal, at that. If, however, I was to go back to college, the question of how smart I really was needed to be answered. Accordingly, Mr. Thume administered an IQ test to me and settled the issue once and for all. It showed me to be of considerably higher than average intelligence and, thus, not only supported the idea that earning a degree was a reasonable goal for me, but that graduate work might be appropriate as well. Needless to say, that was welcome information and a boost to my ego.

With the positive reinforcement I was getting on various fronts, my self-confidence began to soar. Dr. Payton Kolb, the center psychiatrist, noticed the changes occurring in me and called me into his office one day to tell me how pleased he was with me. When I left him, it was a wonder I didn't have the big head. Actually, I think I did.

Linda Jean was able to come up for a visit during this period and was delighted to find I was progressing on all fronts. She had helped care for me and knew all too well the terrible shape I had been in. Consequently, seeing my old cockiness return was a real joy to her. She also got to meet a number of my friends at the center and was able to spend quite a little bit of time with my good buddy, Frank Clifford. When she left the center after her visit, she did so with a feeling that things were going to work out OK for me.

Throughout the fall I continued to make steady progress in cane travel, eventually reaching the point where I had completed all the assignments in Little Rock. This was quite an accomplishment and one that was realized by very few trainees. The very fact that I stayed at the center longer than most partially accounted for it, but that wasn't the whole story, a realization which gave me a good deal of self-satisfaction.

Since I had training time remaining, Mr. Burke sent me to find addresses in north Little Rock, a town I'd never even visited. As a consequence I had no idea that shortly after I crossed the street separating Little Rock from North Little Rock I would be over what I later learned was a viaduct. All I knew at the time was that there was something different about my surroundings, and it gave me a feeling of uneasiness. Cars were whizzing by on my left quite close, so I tried hard to keep to the right side of the sidewalk. There was a rail on that side that suggested I was on a bridge, but I didn't know that for sure. What I did know was that something was preventing me from being confident that I was in complete control of myself. The obstacle perception that had so recently been helpful to me in maintaining a sense of equilibrium all of a sudden seemed to be playing awful tricks on me. Despite my efforts to prevent it from happening, I continually felt that the ground was shifting under my feet and though I knew it was foolish, I felt as if I was in danger of falling into what seemed like an abyss on the other side of the rail. Over and over I tried to tell myself that I was all right, but these efforts provided little relief. Down deep I knew I was scared and I was cursing the blindness that had caused it. I was experiencing a vulnerability unlike anything I had ever known. As a result, I dreaded every step I took, but knowing there was nothing else I could do, I kept walking. I reasoned that it couldn't possibly be long before I'd be on firmer ground somewhere ahead of me and there was no way in hell I was going to let myself turn around and go back. That would have meant failure and I could not have lived with myself if I gave up. Drawing on whatever courage I had left, I pressed on, putting one foot in front of the other, tapping that damn cane as I went.

Mercifully, a few seconds later I felt a change occur and knew that I had made it to the other side. Relief surged through my body, and I could feel my heart rate slow. Never had the simple act of standing on a normal sidewalk felt so good. Feeling that I both needed to and wanted to, I stood long enough to get myself settled down. Then I pulled out my list of addresses and started walking. Mr. Burke told me how the town was laid out, so I knew how I needed to proceed.

A few minutes later, I was sitting in a café, drinking a Coke and getting myself even more under control. Having a Coke always seemed to have that affect on me. Besides that, the young waitress who was serving me seemed like she might be friendly.

After my visit to North Little Rock, Mr. Burke sent me both to Conway and to Pine Bluff. Not only was each town completely new to me, each contained the additional challenge of a round trip by bus.

During both of those assignments, an unusual incident occurred that has stayed with me a lifetime. In Conway, the lady who was my waitress when I had lunch wound up being on the same bus as I on my return trip to Little Rock. By then I had spent several hours locating addresses and making a personal visit to an old agriculture teacher who was a great supporter of the center. Imagine my surprise when my waitress friend boarded the bus and spoke to me. I found it to be extraordinary, but by her demeanor I could tell that it didn't occur to her to think of it as being even remotely unusual.

In Pine Bluff I had the unusual experience of being referred to as being a strawberry blond by a nice young woman working in a department store I was required to locate. Not being satisfied to simply observe to me that she liked my hair, she called a colleague over and pointed out to him the fact that my hair was striking. Never before nor since has anyone made such an observation. Perhaps she thought I needed to be cheered up by having someone brag on me. If so, it worked, but I also wondered about her ability to distinguish color. I remembered quite clearly that my hair was brown, nowhere near blond, strawberry or otherwise.

One other trip I made toward the end of my tenure at the center also stands out in my memory. This one, however, was not an assignment. It was a visit I made to Columbia City, Indiana, with my buddy Frankie Clifford and his parents when his time at the center was over.

In route, we stopped at a small town in rural Illinois where we visited for a day and night with some of Frankie's relatives. For the first time in my life, I went to a skeet shoot. We were far enough away from the guns so that the noise level was tolerable, and I had the additional distraction of three young girls who thought my southern accent was charming and made no bones about it. I was pleased to find that they weren't too badly put off by my blindness either.

Frankie and his parents entertained me nicely the two days I spent in their home, and I've always been glad I chose to visit them. Frankie's life was destined to be short, and he and I both knew it. That visit was the last time we were together.

On my return trip to Little Rock, I went by train. It was the second time I had chosen that means of travel, and it was a whole lot more enjoyable than the first. Thinking back on it, I know that Mrs. Clifford talked a young woman into watching out for me, but at the time, I just thought that lady was being nice, and I certainly did enjoy her company. It was also nice to have her assistance in getting to the dining car for my first meal on a train. What fun!

Two other experiences from that trip also stand out. The first one concerned a fourteen-year-old boy who struck up a conversation by asking what had happened to me. Just as I was starting to tell him about my accident, his mother cautioned him to leave me alone. I had not been bothered by the boy's question, but I certainly was bothered by the behavior of his mother. She had chosen to act as if I didn't even exist. She spoke only to her son, even after I had indicated I didn't mind his questions. Perhaps that wasn't the first time in my life I had been ignored, but it stands out in my memory as a very unpleasant experience. Her unmistakable message was that I was unworthy of her attention. I would have been no more offended if she had spat on me.

The second incident occurred when I had to change trains. A young physician assisted me from getting from one to the other, but, for some reason, I could not engage him in conversation. As we walked, I attempted to show what a friendly fellow I was by asking a few questions. To my dismay, his responses did not seem even remotely friendly. He was willing to help me but unwilling, it seemed, to talk to me. If it was his intention to hurt my feelings, he succeeded quite well.

In early November, a month and a half before I was scheduled to leave the center, I had the pleasure of meeting a young man who would play a very important role in my life. His name was Jim Cordell, and eventually he became a very successful director of the center that is now called Lions World Services for the Blind. Jim, as I was permitted to call him since he and I were about the same age, began his career as a travel instructor, and when Mr. Burke introduced him to me, he said, "You may have to run to keep up with this fellow." We all laughed when he said that, but there was some truth to it.

Jim endeared himself to me very quickly by giving a glowing report to Mr. Burke one day following one of my downtown assignments. Of special interest to him was the fact that I was willing and able to negotiate my way through a construction site that had caught me completely by surprise. I virtually preened as Jim told how well I had handled myself.

Throughout my time at the center I had managed to maintain a friendly relationship with virtually all of the other trainees and as my time for departure drew near, several of them made Christmas gifts for my relatives. My time and talents enabled me to make a couple of rugs and two small cedar chests, but numbers of other gifts were made for me by my fellow trainees.

A few days before I left the center, I was given one final opportunity to help round out my training. Mr. Kumpe gave me a chanced to further hone my public speaking skills by making a brief presentation to a group of visiting Lions. My speech was scheduled to last only three or four minutes, but I knew its length was no measure of its importance.

Wanting me to speak from the heart, Mr. Kumpe gave me very little time to prepare but that was fine with me. I knew exactly what I wanted to say and I was pretty sure I knew what they wanted to hear. My plan was a simple and straightforward one. I was going to stand before them and describe how important their efforts were. In words they could not mistake, I was going to tell them that quite literally they were giving large numbers of persons such as I a new lease on life. Then I was going to close by giving them my personal thanks for the wonderful things the center had done for me.

I think everything would have gone as planned had it not been for one thing I failed to take into account. It did not occur to me that after Mr. Kumpe presented me to those Lions by telling them what a spiffy guy I was, I might be so overcome with emotion that I couldn't speak. Nonetheless, that is precisely what occurred. Though I made a yeoman's effort to do so, I couldn't make any words come forth. I knew I was failing Mr. Kumpe and all those Lions who wanted to hear something from me, with some of them even holding out hope that I would not only rise to the occasion but that I would acquit myself handsomely and say something profound. Well, it didn't happen. In fact, nothing happened--nothing other than the fact that I stood there with tears rolling down my cheeks feeling ashamed that I couldn't do what needed to be done. When it finally and painfully became obvious that I wasn't going to be able to give those fellows my speech, I made one last mighty effort to at least say something that might keep me from being a total flop. Thank goodness, I eventually got four words out between the sobs. I said, "Thank you, thank you."

Mr. Kumpe told me later that I had done fine. "How nice of him to say that," I thought. "Who knows, it might even be true."

When I concluded my five months of training, the question that had to be answered was had I met the goal of being adjusted to being blind. In the estimation of those in a position to know, the answer was an unequivocal yes where the physical requirements of adjustment were concerned. On that dimension I had gained enough independence to enable me to meet virtually all of life's daily demands. Simply stated, I could do virtually all of the things required to lead a fairly normal and happy life.

With respect to the emotional dimension of my adjustment, the "yes" response was also appropriate, but the factor of time took on a higher level of importance. Although learning how to walk with a cane and do virtually everything by touch could generally be accomplished in a fairly short period of time, learning how to accept myself as a blind person down deep in my soul could not be accomplished nearly so quickly. Even at the age of 21, I understood that self-acceptance was hard for everybody, and the struggle continues throughout one's lifetime. Up until the age of 20, I was working at the problem of self-acceptance quite literally seeing myself as I was. Soon after I became 20, however, I had to continue the process of self-acceptance under very different circumstances. In important ways, I was still the same person I had been and was becoming, but after my accident, I had to factor in the ever-present importance of my blindness. It made the whole process harder and the goal a little more elusive, but that just meant I'd have to work at things a little more diligently than most people. And it would be that way for the rest of my life.

Chapter 6

Picking Up Where I Left Off

Since I had time on my hands after I left the center, I spent several weeks visiting friends and family both at home and in Jackson. In many ways it was an enjoyable time but, of course, there was sadness too. Down deep, I had to admit that I missed seeing all of the colors I associated with Christmas, but I tried to focus on the things that were really important to me rather than dwell on what had been lost. To even a close observer, I think I might have appeared to have pulled it off.

A couple of days after Christmas, as I was wrapping up a weeklong visit with Mama and Linda Jean, one of my childhood friends, Bobby Boyd, came to see me. Like many others who dropped by from time to time, he was just checking to be sure I was doing all right, but as I soon learned, there was another reason for his visit. Telling me how he had decided he wanted to do like his brother Wayne and go to Hinds Junior College, he then suggested that the two of us ought to be roommates. I accepted his offer and smiled to myself as I thought about how three and a half years earlier Wayne and I had gone off to Hinds together, also to be roommates.

Before he left, Bobby and I also shared individual memories of being the shoeshine boys in the barbershop. Having an opportunity to regularly be in the company of men such as Leroy Tumey, Edwin Hutto, and Walter Lusk was a great benefit to each of us. We also made a little money. In fact, as I mentioned to Bobby, one Saturday I shined a hundred pairs of shoes for a total of $15. True, it was a 16-hour day, but I still had that $15 in my pocket. I surely was tired, though. Sweeping up all that cut hair and doing the other things that a shoeshine boy had to do in addition to his main work meant he would be plenty busy on a day when the shop was regularly filled with customers.

Being around men from throughout the county and an occasional outsider was also very interesting and, occasionally, even instructive. As I shined shoes, swept and mopped the floor, and picked up the used towels, I kept my ears tuned to what was being said and noted how men from markedly different walks of life interacted with one another. Among the many things I learned from those many hours I spent in the barbershop was that the people of Amite County are fascinating to watch. Just about the time you think you have them figured out, one of them will say or do something that sends you straight back to the drawing board.

More importantly, I had learned firsthand that the people of Amite County will support you well when you need their help. I started to tell Bobby that money had been collected for me several months before in a box strategically placed in the barbershop, but he already knew about it. In fact, as he admitted to me, he had made a little contribution to that fund himself. "Well, Bobby," I said, "maybe you'd be interested to know that I put those several hundred dollars to good use." Laughing, he replied that he figured I might have had a few expenses a while back.

Three weeks later, Bobby and I got ourselves registered at Hinds. Interestingly, it was almost exactly one year to the day after my accident. The people in Registration and other areas of the college who happened to see me gave me a warm welcome and tried to assure me they could be called upon any time.

Since I only needed nine hours to complete my work at Hinds, I decided I wouldn't overdo it by taking more than the minimum. The courses I chose were American History under Mr. J. B. Patrick, Sociology under Miss Susan Brown, and Psychology under Mrs. Lucille Keen. The latter two were new faculty members to me, but I had known Mr. Patrick since I started college back in '57.

Initially, Bobby and I were assigned a room in an old dorm named Central. When a vacancy occurred in Southside, a new dorm that was much nicer, we persuaded the administration we were entitled to have that room since I was an upperclassman. At first, there was resistance to the idea because of Bobby being a freshman, but we were persistent and the folk at Hinds didn't know that a couple of guys from Amite County would be likely to be more assertive than most folks. That, however, was another thing he and I had learned along the way. If you want something, the best thing to do is go after it and don't stop until you get it.

Southside was a much nicer dorm than Central and had the great benefit of having a bathroom that had to be shared only with four other fellows. Its only disadvantage was that it was pretty far removed from the main part of campus, and I didn't have much to guide by in getting to and from it. Bobby, or someone else from the dorm, was typically around if I needed help, but I still was always a little uncomfortable when I thought about the fact I might get lost.

With the tremendous turnover in students that occurs each year in a college hardly anyone I had known before was still around, but I did have a friend named Jerry Bridgers who lived in Raymond. To my absolute delight, he came to see me soon after I had settled in, and to my further delight, he offered to come and read to me two hours at a time every Tuesday and Thursday evening. Since I had only a print copy of my textbooks, his offer was more valuable to me than he could have known. Rehab for the blind was covering my costs and had bought me a recorder, which was of some use, but the quality of the duplication was fairly poor, and I wasn't organized enough at the time to figure out how to use it to maximum advantage. Thus, without the help of Jerry, I would have been at a tremendous disadvantage. He was a good reader, too. Listening to him was always a pleasure and without his help I absolutely could not have made it through the semester. Bobby read for me occasionally as did a couple of other friends on the weekend once in a while. Jerry provided me the consistent support that enabled me to keep up on a regular basis.

Sometimes when I had to take a test, my instructors would read the questions to me in a private session and listen to my responses. On other occasions, I'd get Bobby to come and write for me as I dictated my answers. At that time I didn't have a typewriter.

I made it a point to never miss a class and to always be attentive to what my instructor said. Miss Brown liked to have a lot of discussion in her class, and I soon established myself as a student on whom she could count for a contribution when she requested it. In fact, oftentimes, much of the class consisted of her asking how we felt about various sociological issues and me serving as the principal spokesperson for the class. For some reason, hardly anyone other than I was willing to speak up. Looking back on it, I suspect many of my classmates resented me talking so much, but at the time it seemed to be the right thing to do. I also believed that Miss Brown appreciated it. In later years, when I was a college teacher myself and had the experience of asking questions to students who were reluctant to provide a response, I felt I understood why Miss Brown was apparently receptive to what I had to say.

Mr. Patrick lectured almost exclusively, but on those rare occasions when he asked a question, I tried to cooperate with him as well. The fact I had never been shy was again proving to be an advantage for me.

Mrs. Keen's class was similar to Miss Brown's in that she encouraged class members to interact with her. In addition, however, she periodically required each of us to make an oral report on an article appropriate to one of the topics we were studying.

Virtually every Friday afternoon, Daddy would pick me up and I would spend the weekend with him and Lucille and my sisters, Sue and Ann. It was something I wanted to do, but even if I had not, I would have still done it. Hinds virtually shut down on the weekend, and I would have been hard-pressed to spend all of those hours in anything like a satisfactory fashion. I had never liked to spend much time alone and being blind didn't change that. In fact, it probably made me even less inclined to be content being by myself for a long period of time. At Daddy's I had the benefit of being with family members and could relax and just be myself. The fact that Lucille was a good cook and would often fix things she knew I liked didn't hurt anything either.

Sue and Ann enjoyed my company and would come to see me often and ask me to play with them. Since Ann was only about two and a half, keeping her entertained for short periods was easy. Her favorite thing for me to do was to catch under her arms and throw her up in the air as high as I could reach.

Despite the trauma to my body, I still had considerable strength in my arms and chest and hurling her or one of her friends high into the air was fun for all concerned. On numbers of occasions, Ann would come rushing up to me with a young friend in tow and say to her, "This is my brother, Jimmy. He's blind and he throws people up." That, of course, was my cue and, in turn, I would grab each of them and "throw them up" with sufficient speed to send their bodies parallel to the ground with them six-and-a-half feet into the air. The sound of their squeals and laughter were like a tonic that could soothe my soul.

Being six years older, Susie often enjoyed somewhat different activities. When her friends would come over and I would join them in a game, I would pretend to be their teacher and we would play school. Susie loved it and could almost always answer whatever question I threw out. Sometimes the other kids could keep up with her for a while but it never lasted. She was too smart for them, and their interest would wane pretty quickly.

Once in a while I got to spend a weekend at home by catching a ride with someone going that way, but more often than not, Mama and Linda Jean would have to come up to Daddy's for us to get in a visit. I knew it was uncomfortable for Mama to be in Lucille's home, but to her credit, she handled it quite well. In fairness, it should be said that Lucille did too. Both Daddy and Lucille typically stayed in the background and kept Susie and Ann occupied elsewhere while Mama, Linda Jean, and I visited in my room.

With Maureen and family living close by, they came out to visit fairly often. For eleven years, Maureen was an only child and there was always a special relationship between her and Daddy, though the divorce had done what I suspect was some irreparable damage. Regardless, when she and Bill and their kids, Billy, Lynn and Mary came, we all visited together, usually including Lucille.

Barbara and Robert, along with their kids, Bobby, Janice and Larry, would come up once in a while from Baton Rouge for a visit, as well. As was the case with me, Barbara had been deeply hurt when Daddy left us, but the hurt wasn't so fresh anymore, and as we all ate and talked and laughed together, we could almost forget about what used to be.

On weekends when no family members came, I would sometimes have a visit from a friend. I was back-page news by then but once in a while a friend would come by to check on me, and we would sit and talk. Those from home knew me the best but even those who were of more recent vintage could still help me to keep my spirits up and find much to be thankful for. Even though my accident had forced more maturity on me than I wanted, I was still only 21 and young enough to just want to live life as if it was supposed to be – fun.

On Sunday evenings when Daddy would drive me back to Hinds, I would often think about what had happened to me only a year before, and on many occasions those memories would send me into deep depression. Within minutes of the time we would leave the house, we would be very close to the place where, as I had named it, the "damned accident," had occurred, and I could almost feel negative vibes coming at me from the place where my car smashed against that dump truck. Even if Lucille, Susie, and Ann had chosen to come with us, I would still feel as if I was completely alone in the world. My stomach would knot up and I would be able to feel the excess acid being involuntarily pumped into it. By the time we arrived at my dormitory on such occasions, I would be ready to throw up.

Thankfully, my courses never did cause insurmountable problems. Even in history, which required the mastery of quite a bit of detail, I was able to maintain a B average. The sociology and psychology courses, by their very nature, were easier for me to manage, and I consistently made A's in them.

My lack of success in other areas, however, often caused me concern. Particularly vexing was my inability to make new friends and fit in. Only one fellow in my dorm was willing to spend any time whatever with me. His name was Donny Ross, and he was a native of South Carolina. Like me, he enjoyed breakfast, and we would often walk over to the cafeteria and eat together. Donnie would also come by my room sometimes just to visit, something virtually no one else ever did.

With the girls, things were even worse. Rarely would one so much as speak to me. Since I had never had that problem before, I knew exactly why they were avoiding me, and I both resented it and was hurt by it. I tried to harden myself against how I was treated, but I usually couldn't do it. Regardless of what I told myself, the sense of loneliness and the sense of exclusion were still there.

My friend, Jerry Bridgers, and I did double-date one time that semester, but I had the distinct feeling my date had gone out with me on a lark. Everything I did or said seemed to invoke no response in her that had any meaning whatever.

For the most part, however, the faculty and staff at Hinds treated me extremely well and rarely let my blindness come between me and them. All three of my instructors showed me respect and my association with them was quite salutary. Mr. and Mrs. Oakes, whom I had known in my first year at Hinds, were remarkably nice to me and, through them, I also gained the friendship of Mike Rabalais, an excellent instructor of psychology. Only rarely did I have an unpleasant encounter, and it would typically be something such as being ignored by a service employee. For example, when I went to the grill for a Coke, as I would step up to the counter to make my order, an unthinking employee would look at someone behind me or beside me and ask that person what I wanted. I occasionally still experience that, and it never ceases to puzzle me. Why would anyone assume that because I am blind it's necessary for someone else to speak for me?

I remember one occasion when it became necessary for me to assert myself and claim a privilege that was rightfully mine. It occurred when the semester was over and plans were being made for the graduation exercise. The Registrar suggested to me it might be better if I sat in a slightly different place than the rest of the graduates. Still close, as she pointed out to me, but not with them, as I noted to her. She persisted in her argument that it would be perfectly appropriate for me to be the only one who didn't walk across the stage to receive his or her diploma. What she had no way of knowing, of course, is that we folk from Amite County also tend to be a little bit hardheaded, although always polite. Speaking to her as pleasantly as I could, I said, "No M'am. I've worked pretty hard to get this far so I'm going to walk across the stage just like everybody else. Don't worry about it, I'll be OK." I could tell she didn't like it, but I hadn't left her much to say on the subject, which, of course, was my intention.

On graduation day I did walk across that stage, tapping my cane as I went, and the President made a special point to speak to me as he handed me my diploma, and I moved on to make room for the next graduate amid a good bit of applause. My family was there, of course, and that made for a good number of clappers not even counting the rest of the audience.

A lot of the faculty came up and congratulated me after the ceremony, and one of them, Miss Brown, gave me a gift – a sociology book that I used for years. All in all, it was a happy day for me and I remember it fondly despite the fact I didn't make a single friend among those with whom I graduated.

I spread the word among my family members that they should all give me money for my graduation rather than a gift of their choosing. Daddy couldn't believe my gall and he told me so with a smile, but I had decided I wanted a suit, and I figured I'd collect enough money from them to buy it. I had several thousand dollars in my checking and savings accounts as a result of the money I was paid by my insurance company for the damage done to my body, but I didn't know how long it would have to last. Thus, it made good sense to me to do what I was doing.

Daddy had always bought Hart, Schaffner, and Marx suits, so he shouldn't have been surprised that I wanted to be in position to put my best foot forward. I knew exactly what I was doing, though. I was moving my life forward, and when I needed to, I would do it wearing a good-looking suit.

Chapter 7

Becoming a College Graduate

After finishing at Hinds I had a few weeks off before I would begin summer school in Hattiesburg at what would soon be called the University of Southern Mississippi. Because of family tradition it was a foregone conclusion that's where I would go. It was founded as Mississippi Normal College but by the time Daddy graduated from there in 1937, the name had long since been changed to State Teachers College. Maureen followed in Daddy's footsteps a dozen years later, by which time the name had been changed to Mississippi Southern College. Interestingly, if things went the way I hoped, I would be earning my degree after little more than another dozen years and a final name change. Knowing I was following Daddy's and Maureen's lead caused some excitement for me, but I was also intimidated. Simply stated, I wasn't sure I could measure up.

Wanting always to spend as much time as I could at home, I took advantage of my reprieve to see Mama and Linda Jean. For several days I mostly just sat around and visited with them and an occasional friend who dropped by. Invariably we would talk about the funny and crazy things we had done and laugh at our own foolishness, or try to.

Linda Jean was working as usual, but that time it was for the purpose of having college money. She had made her plans to join me in the fall at Southern, along with boyfriend Charles Carruth. Daddy had asked her to live with him and go to Hinds her first two years the way I had done, but that just wasn't what she wanted to do. As a consequence she was going to have to, very largely, fend for herself. I felt badly about the position she found herself in but was still happy she and I would be going to college together.

As always Mama was proud of what her children were doing, and although I'm sure she dreaded the prospect of her last child leaving home, she never let on. The fact that none of us would be more than a two-hour trip away was probably also comforting. Both Maureen and Barbara Ann visited often enough for her to be reassured of her importance, and I'm sure she knew Linda Jean and I would do the same thing.

Finally deciding I had put it off long enough, it was also during that visit home when I decided to make my solo walk from home to town. I needed to let people know I still had my independence, but I surely did dread what lay before me. Even though I had a perfect mental image of the whole area, I knew it would not be easy to go to all the places I wanted to without making any number of false steps.

Our home was located squarely behind the county courthouse only 20 feet back from the street. If I crossed straight ahead from my sidewalk I would easily find the sidewalk leading to the court house, and I would be perfectly oriented. The fact that the street was fairly wide was a major consideration, but, as I said to myself as I approached it and hoped for the best, "That's the way it is."

Falling into my old pattern my aim wasn't completely true, but it was close enough for me to find the path leading to the sidewalk without making too much of a spectacle of myself in the unlikely event anyone was around to see me. A couple of minutes later I stepped up on the porch at the back of the courthouse and headed for the door, which I knew to be open because of the sounds coming through it. As soon as I stepped inside, Mr. Hylon Whittington came up and spoke to me. I think I would have recognized his voice, but since I heard the characteristic thump of his limp when he approached, I didn't need to. He and I chatted for a moment and got caught up on one another's news. It had been my plan to go into all of the offices and speak to as many people as I could, but they apparently heard me talking and decided to save me the trouble. At any rate, I was able to follow the line of least resistance and just speak to various friends as they came up.

After I had greeted everyone, making my way through the courthouse and ultimately down to Main Street presented no problem other than the necessity of avoiding the flagpole strategically placed right in the middle of the sidewalk. I made sure my cane tapped the pole so I knew exactly where it was. There was no doubt in my mind I was being watched by several friends from the courthouse, and I was determined to not embarrass myself. Ordinarily I would have had memories of playing football and baseball with my buddies on that part of the court square just to my right, but on this occasion I was concentrating too precisely on swinging my cane in just the right arc.

When I reached the end of the sidewalk I had to wait only for a moment before I could cross. Traffic in Liberty was never heavy even on Main Street. Figuring there would be enough auditory cues when I got close to Blalock's, I crossed the street with more than a little confidence. As I had hoped would be the case, a man came out of the store just as I was stepping up on the curb. "Hello, Mr. Robertson," he said. I knew instantly it was my old friend R. C. Robbins. He had been one of Daddy's teachers at the Negro school, and his memories of those days were still keen in his mind. We reminisced for a few minutes, and then he held the store door open for me so that I could easily enter. By then Mr. Walter Blalock had seen me from his station at the meat counter and was giving me a hug even before Professor Robbins got the door closed. With obvious pleasure in his voice he told me how glad he was to see me out and about and then proceeded to bring me up to date on everybody. As Mr. Walter knew, all of the Blalocks were my friends, and he took pride in being able to serve as their spokesman. A couple of them called my name as they went about their duties in the store, but they didn't stop their work. They had to keep the business going, and besides that they knew Mr. Walter would say everything that needed to be said.

Fifteen minutes later, Mr. Walter helped me back to the sidewalk and gave me a farewell hug to send me on my way. A minute later, however, I stopped at the hardware store so I could talk with Louis Marsalis. His brother-in-law, Herbert Gordon, was off that afternoon, but business was slow enough for the two of us to visit several minutes without interruption.

I felt especially close to him because he had lost his only son, Robert, in an automobile accident, and I suspected sadness was his constant companion. Besides that, I had dated his daughter, Linda Lou, several times before she started going with Quinn Tony, whom she later married.

Mrs. Nunnery must have had a customer because when I reached her store a moment after ending my pleasant chat with Mr. Marsalis, she didn't come out to speak to me. Since the door was open, though, I spoke as I passed by and made my way to the curb. I was nervous about crossing that street because right then there was no traffic and, thus, no auditory cues to provide any guidance. With nothing else to do, however, I squared myself up and started walking. In seconds I knew I was in trouble. Nothing felt right, but I couldn't decide if I needed to go more toward the right or more toward the left. "Damn," I said to myself as I felt the inevitable tension in my arms and shoulders. I knew I was about to make a fool out of myself and there didn't seem to be anything I could do to keep it from happening. Just then, however, to my relief, and more so to my embarrassment, Mrs. Nunnery came charging up from behind and grabbed me by the arm. She said, "Jimmy, you're in the middle of Main Street. Where on earth are you trying to go?"

"Up to the drugstore, Mrs. Nunnery. I want to stop off there before going to see Mama."

"Well, come on," she said, pulling me along. "I'll get you straight."

Feeling lower than a toadstool, I let her guide me over to the sidewalk I had been trying so hard to find.

With it being in the center of town and generally pretty busy, I knew I wouldn't have any trouble finding the door to the drugstore but I was so rattled by what had just happened I still waged a struggle with myself every step I took. As I had hoped, things improved only a moment later because Bubba Ratcliff called my name and came charging up to me. Taking me by my left arm, he walked me into the drugstore talking incessantly the whole time. Once inside he served as my host, as well as my guide and within a few minutes I had spoken to ten people I had known all of my life plus a couple of strangers who had stopped in for a moment before continuing their journey to Baton Rouge. Speaking in a voice that could have easily been heard in a foundry, Bubba announced to one and all that I was still doing well and that my blindness wasn't going to keep me from doing what I wanted to do. At that moment I loved him like a brother. In fact, that's the way I felt about him all of his life, which turned out to be all too short. Perhaps his health had already started to fail, but, if so, there was no way of knowing it.

When Bubba was satisfied that I had spoken to everybody I needed to, he guided me over to the M & T Store. Mama walked up and met us as soon as we got inside, and after giving Mama a pleasant greeting and slapping me on the back as a farewell, Bubba left us, no doubt to return to the drugstore where he could tell any newcomers that Jimmy Robertson had just been in and was doing fine.

Though not nearly as loud as he, Mama was every bit as good a hostess as Bubba was a host and soon I had spoken to Mama's employees and my friends Sonny Quin and Lola Tumey, plus several people from out in the county whom I had not known before including a very pleasant old Negro woman. By then it was close to five o'clock, and even though the workday was not nearly over, Mr. Sonny suggested to Mama that she go on home. Without a moment's hesitation she took him up on his offer, and the two of us walked out to her old car arm in arm.

The following Sunday I went to church with Mama and Linda Jean. Even though I was a confirmed Methodist I could still fit in with the Baptists and of course the church was full of lifelong friends of all of us. Quite a few people spoke to me, and I was glad I had gone. By then I had been wearing dark shades for several weeks, and the knowledge that people wouldn't be looking at my eyes made me feel less self-conscious. In a way I believe I was hiding behind those shades, but wearing them still gave me a little additional security.

Early that afternoon following a good fried chicken dinner, Mama and Linda took me back to Daddy's. It wouldn't be but a few days until I'd have to start summer school, and I had to get myself ready.

When I had finally gotten everything done and it was time to go to Hattiesburg, Daddy got Susie to ride down with us so he would have good company on the way back. Knowing it would be a pretty full day and hot as well since it was June, we departed Jackson at 7:30 a.m. after a full Robertson breakfast of grits, eggs, bacon, and biscuits. Daddy didn't like to leave home without being fortified and neither did I.

Having the kind of personality he did and always knowing the value of what in our family was simply called "politics," our first visit at Southern was the office of Dr. W. D. McCain, the college president. His assistant General Roger Johnson and secretary Jessie Morrison were there as well, of course, and Daddy assured I got the same warm welcome from them that I got from Dr. McCain. No one was as smooth as Daddy when it came to handling people. In that same office not too many years earlier, he had introduced Maureen to Dr. McCain's predecessor and secured for her a position as student secretary before he left.

After we got me registered at the Student Services Building I was assigned a room in Scott Hall, one of only a few dormitories needed for the summer quarter. We drove down to it, and all three of us carried some of my things as we made our way inside and located my room. On our second trip from the car the proctor came up and said Susie ought not to be in the dorm since she was a girl. Speaking to him in a friendly but still firm voice, Daddy told him that since she was eight years old it would be okay. Susie was a little embarrassed by the incident, but Daddy assured her she hadn't done anything wrong. For my part, I smiled to myself and enjoyed a brief moment without tension.

With all of my things in my room, including the nice suit I'd bought for myself as a graduation gift from all of my family, Daddy began to get me oriented. The dorm itself was no problem, of course, but, as I soon discovered, the route up to the main front of the campus would be something of a challenge. Not only would I have to make a number of turns, in some instances close concentration would be required for me to know when they occurred. With no visual memories to guide me as had been the case at Hinds, I'd have to construct a fresh image of Southern's campus. Daddy wasn't the best in the world at giving verbal directions, but we walked from the dorm up to the cafeteria and the other major buildings enough times for me to feel reasonably confident I could do it by myself without getting lost.

When we took a break for lunch, we crossed Hardy Street which runs along the front of the campus, to a restaurant called Jimmy Faughn's Buffeteria. Daddy and Jimmy were old friends, and as was often the case with me I inherited yet another of Daddy's friends. Jimmy was polite and gracious and tried to make me feel comfortable by saying I should come there any time and have a meal with the certain knowledge he would have a staff ready to meet my needs.

Back on campus we resumed my orientation efforts and stayed at them until Daddy cried "Calf rope." By then we had walked quite a distance, and he was about played out. To tell the truth I was too, and I suspect Susie had enjoyed about as much as she could stand. Thus when we made one final trip down to Scott Hall, they made their departure. That time when Daddy told me good-bye, I'm pretty sure he didn't cry. I didn't either. By then, I had accepted the fact that new things would always be a little tough for me and I'd just have to brace-up. Susie rubbed her nose across my chest as she gave me a good-bye hug, but I don't think she was wiping away tears. Perhaps her mind had shifted to the future and she was thinking about how it might not be too long before she'd be coming down to Hattiesburg to get her college career under way and continue our family tradition one more time.

After Daddy and Susie left, I got busy and arranged everything to my satisfaction. Getting oriented was no problem since the room was small and everything was in a straight line. From the door there was the closet, the study area, and the bed. In less than an hour everything was in order, and I had only worked up a small sweat. For all I knew there might have been an air-conditioned dorm on campus but to my considerable regret, mine wasn't. Keeping the door open helped the air to circulate a little but not much. At least, I thought as I checked the Braille watch that I'd been given at the center and found that it was 4:30, it won't be too long and I'll be having supper in an air-conditioned building. Thinking about supper, however, was a little unsettling because right then I couldn't remember exactly all the turns I would have to make to get to the cafeteria.

Often I found that if I could relax and let my head clear, whatever problem

I was facing could be thought through, and I would feel better. Accordingly I slipped off my shoes and lay down. For a moment there was enough coolness in the bed to make me a little more comfortable, and I could tell I was getting back under control.

Perhaps I dozed off for a few minutes because the next time I checked my watch I found it was after 5:00. Taking one final large breath I rolled off my bed and hit the floor. Conscious always of my personal hygiene, I washed my hands at the lavatory located exactly in the middle of the back wall, and then headed out. Hearing the sound of the TV coming from the lobby, I decided to stop by and see if anyone was there who might be about ready to go to supper. Being gregarious I would have liked to have had company, but being honest with myself, I also knew what I wanted was someone who would be willing to help me get from the dorm to the cafeteria. As I stepped into the lobby I asked in a fairly loud voice if anyone there was going to the cafeteria anytime soon. I paused after speaking and waited to see if I would have any luck. At first I thought the TV was playing to an empty room, but then I heard a sound that suggested someone might be present. Accordingly, I asked again if anyone was there who was going to the cafeteria. After a moment a fellow with a fairly unusual accent spoke up and said that he'd be going pretty shortly if I wanted to wait. A few minutes later I learned that the reason my companion and soon to be friend Jim Selby talked the way he did was that he had spent a good bit of his life in the Panama Canal Zone. I learned that interesting fact and various others as we walked up to the cafeteria together, with him offering a couple of suggestions about landmarks for me to look for. Once we were inside Jim very unobtrusively provided enough cues for me to find a tray and silverware and move down the serving line without incident. A couple of girls were just ahead of us and they flirted with him a little and were friendly toward me as well. When we had finished eating, we took our trays and left them at the receiving window. I had noted its location earlier and could have found it without Jim's help, but being with him made it even easier.

Outside the cafeteria Jim asked if I could get back to the dorm by myself. When I assured him I could, he said he was going to do a little girl watching up at Wimpy's, the campus snack bar hangout. "Good for you," I said as he bade me good-bye and headed out.

He and I met on other occasions before he wound up his studies at the end of the fall quarter of '62. Each encounter was pleasant, and I thought of him many times across the years. Remarkably, as I recently learned, he had thought of me on numerous occasions as well. I learned this surprising fact as a result of receiving a call from his sister, Ginny Entrekin, a long-time friend of mine from church. She explained how Jim described an old classmate whose name he could not recall, but as Ginny concluded, must undoubtedly have been me. After getting an enthusiastic confirmation from me that I was, in fact, the fellow her brother had befriended, she gave him my phone number. Shortly thereafter he and I, in a 30-minute long distance call, easily picked up where we had left off a little less than 46 years ago.

Though it never would have occurred to me that it might be so, the cafeteria proved to be a very special place for me. In only a few days the very lovely ladies who worked the serving line started looking out for me. They quickly learned not only my name but also my preferences. After that, if chicken livers, for example, were on the menu I could always count on having them in abundance. After all these years I remember with clarity the pleasure I got in being called by name or hearing one of them say, "Hello, Baby, we have some of your favorites today." Most of them are gone now, but I ran into one not long ago and the years melted away as she said, "Tell me, Baby, how have you been doing?" Few things have ever been better for my soul.

When I got back to my room after that first meal, I turned on my radio and listened to music until 9:00. Then I got up, stripped off my clothes, slipped on my robe, grabbed a bar of soap and a towel, and made my way down the hall to the shower room. Daddy had done a good job in getting me oriented to everything, so a few minutes later I was back in my room, clean and refreshed.

As I lay in my bed that first night and took stock of things before I went to sleep, I found to my delight that I wasn't scared. A brand-new experience would start the following day, but I felt I was ready for it.

Arising early the next morning, I made my way back to the cafeteria by

7:00 a.m. so I would have plenty of time for a relaxed breakfast. That had always been my favorite meal, and I didn't like to rush it. As I had hoped, all of the foods I liked were available to me in abundance. Fifteen minutes after arriving I had experienced the pleasure of having bacon, grits, and eggs and was on my way back to my room to brush my teeth. "So far, so good," I told myself as I tried to ignore what seemed to be a little tightness in my stomach.

With time to spare, since it was only a block from the cafeteria, I made it to College Hall where I would have Dr. Stritch for Child Psychology. I had found the introductory course in Psychology to be very interesting, and the idea of following it up with a course that focused on children was appealing. Also, as I discovered a few minutes later, Dr. Stritch was going to make the course not only interesting but more than a little challenging.

My next class was Applied Psychology under Mr. Gurman. Since it was scheduled for the George Hurst Building just down the street from College Hall I was able to get to it early as well. Once again I took a chair in the front of the room. I had learned long before that most students didn't like to be up there, but it was ideal for me.

Mr. Gurman wasn't nearly as dynamic as Dr. Stritch, but his knowledge of the subject was apparent, and I had every reason to believe Applied Psychology would be as interesting as Child. Learning how the findings of this fairly new discipline could be used in fields such as business and education struck a responsive chord in me, and I listened very intently as Mr. Gurman described how the course would unfold.

My third and final course was Educational Sociology under Dr. John Burrus, and the prospect of being able to compare what I learned under Mr. Gurman about the influence of psychology on education with what I learned from Dr. Burrus about the influence of sociology on education was intriguing. Similarly I was looking forward to building on the knowledge I had gained from Miss Brown about the field of sociology. The only problem with Dr. Burrus' course was that finding the sociology building wasn't easy, but a good Samaritan type named Ron Young saw my plight and offered to be my guide until I had completely learned my way around. What a nice fellow he was.

Soon after the quarter got underway, I began to make a few friends from my classes as well as the dorm. That made my life considerably more comfortable, and I began to feel like a real part of the college. Within a few weeks I had also met Denson Napier, the head of the Methodist student organization called the Wesley Foundation and was joining him and a nice little collection of students in various activities. I had attended church several times since my accident, but that was my first real opportunity for regular participation in religious services. Denson was a very open and receptive-type person, and he and I established an easy friendship. Since his wife was from Wilkinson County and knew many of my people, I immediately made friends with her as well.

Throughout the summer I felt good about the progress I was making except for my class performance. I was steadily getting myself reestablished as a "C" student, in spite of all my efforts to keep it from occurring. I didn't want my professors to have that image of me, but it seemed inevitable that they would. I was trying hard, but success was still eluding me. As yet, I had not found a strategy that would enable me to rise to the intellectual level I needed to achieve in order to stop merely being mediocre. I never missed a class, and I was always attentive. I also spent as much time in outside preparation as I could manage, but these efforts were not enough. What I needed was some way to synthesize the material I was required to master, but try as I might, I couldn't do it. Not right then, anyway.

By the time the end of the summer came, I was actually relieved to have made a "C" in each course. For a while it had appeared my grades were going to be a real embarrassment. Even so, I was disappointed with myself and more than a little perplexed. Neither my rehab counselor nor anyone else criticized me, and it was a good thing they didn't. I was on a short fuse, and I didn't need anybody to tell me that I hadn't quite measured up.

When I returned to campus in the fall I was all rested up and ready to prove I could do better than I had done the previous quarter. "Things are going to be different," I told myself. Whatever it took I was determined to make it so.

When I returned for my second quarter, I found a number of things were not like they had been. Most striking among the changes was the presence of a great many more students. They were everywhere. Among them, thank goodness, were Linda Jean and Charles. Though I knew our different schedules would prevent us from spending much time together, their very presence was a source of comfort to me, and I knew if I needed them they could be counted on without question.

Another major change for me was that of being reassigned from Scott Hall to what was called West Stadium. As suggested by the name, the rooms of West Stadium were built under the seats of the football arena. From the perspective of location it was ideal, but it also held another great advantage for me – it was the dorm to which members of the football team were assigned. That meant I would be thrown into regular contact with them, and if my hopes were realized, my circle of friends would be broadened and made considerably more diverse.

The luck of the draw being what it was, the three of us who were assigned to room 17 happened to be named James and often were called Jim. As unlikely a coincidence as that was bound to gain attention, and it did. Soon we were known among large numbers of our fellow students as the three Jims from West Stadium. To avoid confusion we called one another by our last names. The youngest of us was Kitchens from Crystal Springs, a beginning freshman destined to become a lawyer. I was next in age, followed by LaPointe from Bay St. Louis who was later to become a professor in southwest Louisiana.

If I had assumed that the football players would be a bunch of meatheads, I was wrong. Several of them were quite bright and went on to become very successful in teaching, business, and even medicine. More importantly, many of them were exceptionally nice fellows. Included among those was Nick Kolinsky, a friend of mine to this day.

Through Linda Jean I met a professor who came to play an important role in my life very quickly. Her name was Jessie Wall. In many ways she gave new meaning to the term "unusual." But in even more ways she gave new meaning to the term "lovely." For some reason she decided to take me on as a project, and, having done so, she set out to not only find me a place where I could study in peace and have people to come and read to me, she also decided to find the readers.

Being an Episcopalian she knew that the room in the Student Union building set aside for the Episcopal student organization called the Canterbury Club wasn't being regularly used. Reasoning that it would be a good spot for me, she made all the necessary arrangements for me to have almost exclusive use of the room and then presented me with a key.

For reading volunteers she turned to the local Jewish Sisterhood and to the Hattiesburg Chapter of the Junior Auxiliary. Both groups responded quite favorably, especially the Sisterhood, and soon I had volunteers reading to me virtually every free hour I could manage. Most of them were college graduates, and they rarely stumbled over the technical terms that appeared frequently in my textbooks.

Soon many of the ladies who spent all of their time reading to me became my close friends. They not only shared their time and talents with me, some of them such as Dottie Stetelman even opened their homes to me. Knowingly or not, they also helped me to grow as a person not just as a student.

Though most of the ladies who started reading to me back then are gone now, happily some of them still live, and I count them among the best friends I've ever had. In deference to those who belonged to the Sisterhood, I occasionally attend services at the Temple, and when old friends such as Lou Ginsberg, Shirley Gurwitch, or Betty Reuben see me I always get a hug. If there are worshipers nearby who do not know me, they will be called over so that I can be introduced as a fellow who was helped by the Sisterhood to eventually earn three degrees.

With Mississippians tending to stay put as they do, another close friend, Mary Montague, who started reading to me in '61 as a member of the Junior Auxiliary, still lives in Hattiesburg, and we too find opportunities to visit with one another. Often, of course, our conversations turn to instances of the past, many of which give us a chuckle. Once for example, back in '62, when Mary saw me on campus as she was running late for one of her own classes, she deliberately whizzed by me without speaking. To her surprise, I called to her retreating figure and said, "Well, Mary, aren't you going to visit with me?"

"No," she said, "I don't have time, but tell me how did you recognize who I was?"

"I smelled your perfume," I said.

For the record it was Arpege, and if my memory serves me correctly, its wonderful slogan of the time was, "Promise her anything, but give her Arpege." If it wasn't, it ought to have been.

With the help of Sisterhood and the Junior Auxiliary I had hopes of doing better in the fall than I had in the summer despite the fact I was taking 16 hours. Still thinking that I might have a professional interest in Sociology as well as Government and Psychology, I took Social Institutions in addition to Public Administration, Social Psychology, and Abnormal Psychology.

As had been the case before, all but one of my professors had a Ph.D. and also, like before, the one lacking that degree would soon overcome his handicap. I continued to be in awe of people who were so smart and so well educated; an inclination that didn't always serve me well. My mind tended to freeze-up when I considered what they knew and what I didn't know.

That fall I also found a young woman who was willing to read for me professionally for the pitifully small amount of money Rehab was willing to pay. Her name was Fay Browne, and she proved to be an excellent reader. Of course she would have been by virtue of the fact that she was a graduate of the University of Chicago at the age of 14. She entered that grand institution when she was only 11 and passed over a year's work by taking tests. As would be imagined, she had read very widely and, as a consequence, was able to provide me with expert tutoring upon occasion.

To my dismay, despite all of the additional help I was receiving, I managed to earn only a "B" in Abnormal Psychology. No doubt in partial compensation for that fact, but still to the amusement of my family and friends, I observed that I had learned a great deal about myself in that course but even more about them.

It also happened that I made another lifelong friend as a result of having taken Abnormal Psychology. His name is Jerry Sullivan, and he now lives in Memphis, Tennessee, where he spent his career in college teaching. As I told him many times, I'm glad he put his brain to good use.

Other than my slight disappointment with my academic performance,

I felt the fall quarter was a rousing success. I had made a large number of friends among my fellow students and, as a result of all of the ladies who read to me, quite a few friends from in town as well. My confidence and my competence seemed to be growing, and I usually felt good about myself. Some people still avoided me, and I would occasionally be made to feel out of place, but these incidents were sufficiently rare as to go almost unnoticed.

In addition to the other good things that were happening to me, I was enhancing myself socially by being seen fairly regularly in the company of several good-looking coeds. Soon after the quarter began, one of them, an especially pleasant girl from Pascagoula named Margaret Doescher, became a regular companion. My friends and family reported to me that she was very attractive and being seen with her didn't hurt my reputation at all. Her company was enjoyable, and no one could have been any more helpful to me than she was. Very often she happily walked to class with me, even when it was necessary for her to go well out of her way.

For reasons unclear to me at the time, or later for that matter, the winter quarter of '62 proved to be the best of my career. I made one "A," two "Bs," and one "C," with the latter grade being in Logic, the hardest course I ever took anywhere. I still have an occasional nightmare involving syllogisms. That course started with 40 of us enrolled in it and ended with a total of ten. My major professor, Dr. Leon Wilber, had gotten permission for me to take Logic as a substitute for the Math requirement, which I thought was a wonderful idea at the beginning of the quarter. Soon thereafter, however, I wondered to what extent he had done me a favor. Even so, I did receive what I considered to be a high compliment from my professor, Jerry Bishop, as I was taking his final exam. He was in earshot of me as I dictated my answers to Fay Browne so she could record them in the strange fashion required in a Logic course. Once as Mr. Bishop got up to take a break from his work, he stopped long enough to exchange a word with me. Speaking in his very precise fashion, he said, "Mr. Robertson, I perceive that you have learned some logic." With sweat dripping off my hands as I stood, I said, "Thank you, Mr. Bishop. I believe your perception is correct." Fay Browne laughed, and I tried to join her, but I knew I still had truth tables to deal with.

Toward the end of that quarter I also passed what was called the English proficiency test. It was designed to screen out students who needed some remedial help in the fundamentals of writing. Presumably, anyone who didn't fit that category would get through the test fairly easily. Happily, that proved to be the case with me.

To pass, all a student had to do was to write either an acceptable six-hundred-word essay or two three-hundred-word essays. To assure standardization, you had to choose from a list of topics provided for you at the beginning of the test. Knowing what a lousy typist I was, I got the English department to give me permission to have Linda Jean type for me as I gave her precise dictation, including punctuation and spelling.

I chose to write a six-hundred-word essay on the subject of procrastination. For a while, Dr. Linwood Orange sat and listened to me as I gave Linda Jean explicit dictation. Eventually, however, he laughingly said on his way out that I obviously didn't need him to monitor what I was doing. I appreciated his honesty and was also glad for him to be gone. His presence made it difficult for me to think.

To Linda Jean's amusement, I sat there and gave her a long and fanciful recitation about what a lovely thing procrastination is. As usual I was full of myself, and it really wasn't difficult at all to compose an essay of only six hundred words. Mrs. Delacey Aaron had taught me English quite well at Liberty High School, and I wound up passing the English proficiency test, just as I knew I would. That success helped to round out the quarter.

It was the next quarter, however, that turned out to be the most important one of all. The reason for its importance lies in the fact it was the one in which I met the girl I was going to marry. Quite naturally it took a while for me to have that realization, but it didn't take very long for me to learn that this girl, among other virtues, had a very quick wit. In fact, I learned that of her as a result of the very first words she ever spoke to me. By chance she and I had both enrolled in Dr. Wilber's International Politics course, and when I entered the classroom on the first day she was already there. As it happened, the fellow who came in just ahead of me was about to take the chair I had occupied the preceding quarter under Dr. Wilber. Seeing what was about to happen, he stopped the fellow from taking my chair by saying, "That's Mr. Robertson's place." As I slipped into the seat just vacated, this cute young thing, who I soon learned was named Linda McSwain, leaned over and asked with laughter in her voice, "How many times have you had this course?" I laughed too, but I didn't think it was as funny as she did. Nonetheless, we hit it off OK on our first meeting and before long we decided to get together and study for our first test.

Our initial study session proved to be a success, based on our respective performances, so we decided to study together regularly. Finding her to be bright and charming, as a result of these sessions, I elected to try to move our relationship to a different level. One day, following our study session, I asked her for a date the following Saturday night. At first she was quite reluctant to say yes, and my heart began to sink, but I screwed up my courage and began to try to talk her into changing her mind. Eventually, to my immense relief, she relented.

To make sure Linda didn't have to be our driver the first time we went out, I made arrangements for us to double date. Even so, I was more than a little anxious as my good buddy, Warren Bradberry from Milton, Florida, and I rode down to Linda's hometown, New Augusta, to pick her up. Among other concerns, the prospect of my having to meet her parents and present myself as a fellow worthy of spending time with their daughter sent a quiver up and down my spine. As it happened, however, I shouldn't have worried so much. Linda met Warren and me at the door, and we left without meeting her dad and mom, Wilfred and Daisy McSwain.

We double-dated a time or two after that, but it wasn't long before another good friend, Fred White, started loaning Linda and me his car on a regular basis. He would drive me to New Augusta to pick Linda up, and when we got back to Hattiesburg she'd take the wheel for our date. At the end of the evening she and I would pick Fred up, and he would take the wheel for our return trip to New Augusta.

From the outset Linda and I got along well, and from our second date on when I met her family, they appeared to accept me well enough. Within six months of the time we first met, it appeared to me we might well have a long future together.

My college work moved along at a good pace too, and although I never achieved distinction in any of my classes, I consistently did at least acceptably well. My interest in both psychology and government or political science, as it was often called, continued, and I wound up with a minor in the former and a major in the latter.

At the end of the summer quarter of '62, I found that I only lacked 20 hours, or five courses, to meet the requirements for a degree. Though that was an extraordinary load, I invoked a senior privilege and took all of them in the fall quarter. At its conclusion I was worn out physically, but exhilarated emotionally.

Chapter 8

Raising the Bar

Though I knew I was in a pretty select crowd when I became a college graduate, I also knew I couldn't rest on my laurels. At some point in my past, perhaps even as early as my time at the rehabilitation center, I began to let myself think of the possibility of graduate school. When that thought first occurred I probably pushed it aside, classifying it as a foolish dream. Somewhere around the mid-point of my bachelor's work, however, I gave my graduate work goal a new classification. I started referring to it as a practical dream, one that I could, in fact, realize. Then, having decided that I could do it, I convinced myself I should do it, perhaps even that I must do it.

If I'd entertained the idea that finding a way to go to graduate school would be easy, I would have been sorely disappointed. When I broached the subject to my rehab counselor, for example, it wasn't well received. In fact, the phrase "It went over like a lead balloon" comes to mind. I shouldn't have been surprised by that and for the most part I wasn't, but on a deeper level I was disappointed. What, I asked myself, do the people in rehab expect me to do? Couldn't they tell that I wasn't the type to be content with the status quo? Weren't they smart enough to know I had the ability to really accomplish something?

For a while my conversations with Dr. Leon Wilber weren't very productive either. As the chairman of the newly created Department of Political Science, he was in a position where he could have been of considerable help, but initially he seemed to be almost bereft of ideas. At one point he did mention Florida

State, but I detected little enthusiasm in him for his own idea. Thinking of it from the standpoint of cost alone I rejected it out of hand.

For a while my situation seemed to be almost hopeless. Not even Daddy could come up with any good ideas. His advice was usually sound, but in this instance, like the rest of us, he just couldn't figure out what to do.

Sometimes, however, things simply work out right, despite the fact it appears impossible that they could. That's what happened to me just before I finished the requirements for a bachelor's degree. The governing board for Mississippi's universities granted USM permission to add another graduate program – a master's degree in Political Science.

I wasted no time in getting myself admitted to the graduate school, and when the winter quarter of the '62-'63 school year began, I signed up for three courses. Continuing the pattern I had begun months before, I worked hard enough to ensure reasonable success. Ten-hour days were common, but twelve-hour days occurred fairly frequently as well. The assigned reading alone required a yeoman's effort, and that was only a part of what was expected of me. By then quite a few books were available on tape, but I still put my friends from the Sisterhood and elsewhere to very good use. Denson Napier, the director of the Wesley Foundation, was kind enough to give me exclusive use of a room in the Wesley building, and I put it to use seven days a week for months on end.

When the spring quarter began, I signed up for additional courses and continued moving toward my goal. As I had done the previous quarter, I confined my social activities to the time I had available, which never was much. Fortunately Linda understood what I had to do, and she never complained about it. Our relationship was serious by then, but we hadn't yet made any definite plans for the future.

Toward the end of the spring I was offered a summer job at Arkansas Enterprises for the Blind. Though I was honored to be given such an opportunity, I was concerned about taking the summer off from my graduate program, so I sought Dr. Wilber's advice. To my immense relief he told me if I continued to work with my usual tenacity, I should be able to finish the next spring even if

I did take off for the summer. With Dr. Wilber's blessings I called Mr. Kumpe back and told him he'd soon have the pleasure of my company.

My job at AEB, as it was called, turned out to be interesting at the very outset. Though I had responsibilities related to all trainees, I was principally involved with the college-prep group. They had come to the center from various parts of the country for the specific purpose of learning skills and strategies that would enhance their likelihood of success as students. As would be imagined, they were bright, enthusiastic, and highly motivated. They took what we on the college-prep staff offered them and ran with it. Not once did I have an occasion to question the wisdom of my decision to be there and help them get ready to do what I had already done. My only regret about any of it was that I had not had a similar opportunity myself.

For a short time I entertained the idea I might have a serious interest in rehab work, but it never took root. Being with my friends such as Oliver Burke, Jim Cordell, Bunk Goodrum, and Roy Kumpe every day of the summer was a true pleasure, but I soon realized an academic career was my dominant interest.

Despite the fact I was having a great time with my work, the high point of my time at the center wasn't related to what I was doing. It was, however, intimately related to my personal life. The event to which I refer was a visit from Linda. Midway through the summer she accepted my offer to come up to the center at my expense and spend a few days.

The reason her visit took on such great importance was that it was a turning point in our relationship. Up until then I wasn't completely convinced she could accept me just as I was. By the time she returned home, however, my concerns had largely been laid to rest. During the three days she was at the center, she was thrown into intimate contact with dozens of blind people from a variety of backgrounds. Some of them were highly capable individuals who could meet life head-on and handle it quite well. Several others, however, weren't quite so fortunate, and a few evoked feelings of deep sympathy, perhaps even pity. Remarkably, Linda was at ease with all of them. I found that ability quite admirable, but more importantly it was instructive. If she could accept people who were much more seriously impaired than I, it seemed reasonable to believe we could build a relationship on the kind of mutual respect I believed to be absolutely essential.

When the summer was over and I returned to graduate school, Linda and I continued to see each other regularly on the weekends. With her having made a good record in USM's College of Education, it had been relatively easy for her to get a good teaching position in Pascagoula. She established a practice of returning home on Fridays so that we could see each other on Saturdays for dates and Sundays for visits.

On one occasion, I was even able to spend a little time with Linda in Pascagoula. She was staying in the home of the mother-in-law of Paul Burke, a minister friend of long standing. In fact both Paul and his wife Lataine were close friends of Linda and her entire family.

Until November 22, I spent a number of very enjoyable hours with Linda and her landlady Mrs. Hollis, and Linda even took me to her school so I could meet her colleagues. With all of those experiences I would have had nothing but fond memories of those days in Pascagoula, but one incident changed everything. I was in Mrs. Hollis' kitchen about to have my lunch when I heard a report of such terrible news I would never be able to get it out of my mind. It was when I learned that President Kennedy had been assassinated.

Although still shaken, I got back into my studies the following week and tried to carry on my life as usual. By then I'd made up my mind I was going to ask Linda to marry me, and I focused my thoughts on that happy prospect as much as I could.

Over the Christmas holidays Maureen took me to downtown Jackson so that I could select an engagement ring for Linda. Being as subtle as I could, I had solicited ideas from Linda about the type of engagement ring she would prefer if anybody ever happened to offer her one, and she'd given me some pretty good suggestions. Armed with them and relying on Maureen's eye for beauty, I made my selection – a solitary diamond large enough to attract favorable notice.

Luck being what it is, when I got back to Hattiesburg my buddy Warren Bradberry happened to see Linda and me together and with great excitement in his voice asked, "Have you given it to her yet?" I feigned nonchalance as

I gave Warren some noncommittal answer and tried, without much luck I'm sure, to divert Linda's attention to something else.

Warren's timing was pretty close, though, because only a few minutes later, at my suggestion, Linda and I went to the Wesley building. I directed her into the chapel because I believed what I was about to do took on a holy quality. A few feet inside the chapel I stopped Linda and put my arms around her for a moment. Then dramatically (or it would have been had I not stumbled against a pew) I stepped back and pulled the ring from my pocket. Opening the box so Linda could admire its contents for a moment, I waited feeling more than a little nervous. Then just before I could get my proposal under way Linda said, "Well, put it on me."

Fancying myself to be something of a Southern gentleman, that day I asked Linda's parents for her hand. I think Linda would have married me even if they had not liked the idea. I suspect they knew it because when I finished making my request the only spoken response came from Mrs. McSwain. Giving her characteristic little laugh she said, "Well, I guess Linda has already made up her mind." Linda's dad, whom I knew to like me quite well, gave us his affirmation a little bit later, and only then did I breathe a complete sigh of relief. I knew that when Linda and I married I'd be taking on the whole bunch, and I wanted all of them to feel as good about Linda's choice as possible.

After our engagement, Linda and I both soon returned to our respective responsibilities and as before spent time together only on weekends. I was still on track to finish my master's program in the spring, but my future after that was uncertain.

Once again it was Daddy who proved to be my best advisor. After learning that I had my heart set on being an academician, he explored all of the options he felt were open to me and then decided USM ought to offer me a job. Like everyone else he was aware that it was growing fast. As he reasoned all of those new students would have to have instructors, and, more to the point, some of them ought to have the pleasure of being under my tutelage.

I, of course, was intimately involved with all that was occurring, but it was Daddy along with my brother-in-law Bill McCarthy, a native of Hattiesburg, who took the most aggressive actions. As would be imagined, not everyone looked forward to the prospect of having me on the faculty, and at least one high-level administrator, Claude Fike, was deeply opposed to the idea. I regretted his position, but what he didn't know was that when Daddy made up his mind that a given thing was going to happen there wasn't much way to stop it.

I think Dr. McCain was generally receptive to the idea of having me around, but he was under pressure from Dr. Fike and others to take a contrary position. I went to see Dr. Fike myself to present my case, but it was to no avail. His conviction was that the university had already done right by me, and I should go elsewhere for employment.

Daddy confined his negotiations to Dr. McCain and called on him several times as new ideas occurred to him. Bill conferred with Dr. McCain some and also with Dr. Wilber, whom he had known for many years.

Things finally came to a head in mid spring when we got some other friends involved. We invited my legislators, Senator John William Powell and Representative Frank Wall, to have a visit with Dr. McCain on my behalf. By happy coincidence John William had a sister who had been placed in a situation similar to mine, and Ole Miss had been willing to give her its cooperation. John William told Dr. McCain all about that and suggested that if what we were requesting could be honored by Ole Miss, he saw no reason why USM should not do likewise. Frank Wall gave strong support to that idea and reminded Dr. McCain of how close he and Senator Powell and all of us had always been to USM. Hearing all of that, there wasn't much else for Dr. McCain to consider.

Shortly thereafter I began the misery of taking my comprehensive examinations. The questions I was asked on the written part of the comps, as they were called, were reasonable, but each of them required me to draw on every bit of knowledge I had acquired and on powers of organization that had never been put to such use.

My friend Lois Kirby read the questions to me and sat there patiently for hours on end as I typed my answers on a portable typewriter. When I finished, I was completely exhausted and not at all certain I had passed. The only thing good about it was that it was over.

A week later I learned that, in fact, I had passed, although certainly not with distinction as I concluded on reading the comments from my committee. Nonetheless, the written part of the ordeal was over. All I had left was my oral exam. To prevent the agony from being protracted, Dr. Wilber set that exam for the following week.

Perhaps it was a little better than the written exam, but not much. Sitting there with the committee members asking me question after question, with my having to satisfy them with answers or suffer Lord knows what consequences, was nerve-racking enough to keep me tied in knots. To make things even worse Dr. Musgrove was present for the purpose of being sure I could handle some questions from a psychologist as well as from political scientists.

When they finally decided they had asked me enough questions, I was excused so they could talk among themselves and decide on my fate. Since we were in College Hall I walked down to the Education Department where Linda Jean was working as a student assistant. She took a moment out from her work to stand there and listen to me lamely observe that I thought I'd passed, but I wasn't sure. Being inclined to always take a positive approach, she tried to assure me things were going to work out fine. I tried to believe her, but I didn't quite succeed. By then my adrenaline had apparently dropped because I began to feel a level of fatigue unlike anything I'd known in quite a while.

In a matter of minutes, thank goodness, Dr. Musgrove came and found me, and his demeanor suggested I had passed. When I walked back into Dr. Wilber's office I was greeted with congratulations and hand shakes all around. There would be a few things to do later, but at that moment I knew I had done something no other person in my family had ever done. I had earned a master's degree.

For the sheer joy of it, I participated in the graduation ceremonies at the end of the spring quarter. Linda Jean had been a great help to me ever since she and Charles had arrived on campus, so I asked her to do me the honor of accompanying me as my degree was conferred. Charles, too, had done me more favors than I could count, and I was delighted he could be there along with my family to witness the good thing he had helped to assure.

A couple of weeks later I went up to Hinds Junior College and let everybody there know about my progress and thanked them for what they had done for me. George McLendon, the president of the college, was especially glad to see me, and upon learning that I had the summer free, asked me if I would like to teach a couple of courses. Without even stopping to think how I would work out the details, I gave him an enthusiastic "Yes!"

A few days later I moved some of my things into a dormitory room at Hinds and began my career as a government instructor. I patterned myself after Dr. Wilber who had let me serve as his teaching assistant and after Dr. William Hatcher who was also my image of what an academician ought to be.

Rehabilitation for the Blind was delighted with what I was doing and showed its pleasure by offering to pay for someone to read for me several hours each week. The person I chose for that important work was Jerry Peyton, who was at that time only fifteen years old. She was quite bright, however, and came highly recommended by Mr. McLendon himself. Jerry proved to be an excellent reader, and we worked extremely well together. Her parents, Liston and Ollie Margaret, also introduced me to Congressman John Bell Williams who would soon alter his career.

When the first term was over I moved right into the second term, but that time I taught state and local government. The training I had gotten at USM served me well again, and judging by my reception among the students, I must have been better than merely adequate.

That summer I got myself reacquainted with several faculty and staff members I had known before and also gained the friendship of Byrle and Mary Jo Kynerd. They had been very popular students at Hinds years before, but at that time our paths had rarely crossed. Through Byrle, I was also able to acquire the friendship of his brothers, Tom and Curtis, and their wives, Nancy and Wanda.

As soon as I finished my obligations at Hinds, I scheduled my long-delayed appointment for the removal of an infected tear sack. That surgery was very important because it represented the last vestige of anything directly associated with my accident. After four and a half years, I figured it was about time.

Chapter 9

Making Other Dreams Come True

As mid-August of 1964 approached my level of excitement grew almost exponentially. Two of the most important events of my life were about to occur, and I could hardly wait. Using the descriptive language of previous generations, I will say that I was about to take a wife. Secondly, I was about to take a job. Or, to state the latter somewhat more elegantly, I was about to take a teaching position.

On August 16, a Sunday, what I had feared would not happen finally did. Linda McSwain said, "I do." Up until then, I couldn't get it out of my mind that something might happen to prevent her from taking that final step. I was ready to take it myself, and when she walked down the aisle toward me, I wanted the expression on my face to reflect that fact. My sisters told me later I had done it. In fact, as they put it, I was beaming.

The service went off flawlessly. Linda and I both spoke up clearly as we repeated the lovely words traditionally used in a Methodist wedding ceremony. Even our exchange of rings went smoothly. I held Linda's hand quite firmly, perhaps to steady my own, as I put the ring on her finger and breathed a great sigh of relief.

Jennings Poole, a friend and former minister of Linda's and a distant cousin of mine, performed the ceremony and handled himself admirably. When Linda and I knelt to take Communion, the holy significance of what we were doing embedded itself in me, and, like John Wesley at Aldersgate, I felt my heart strangely moved.

I got Daddy to be my best man and my friends, Jim and Jimmy Simmons, to be ushers. Linda used her sisters and mine to fill the other positions of responsibility, and we had a very nice reception following the wedding. If Mama and Daddy felt any awkwardness standing in the receiving line being separated only by Linda's mother, they did a good job of concealing it.

A nice crowd of family and friends had come to help Linda and me get our lives together off to a good start. A good number of them hung around long enough to shower Linda and me with rice as we headed for Linda's car to begin our honeymoon.

As Linda drove us toward Jackson, from which we would depart the following morning for St. Louis, I felt the kind of contentment you get when you know you've done the right thing. Quite unexpectedly, the feeling was strengthened when we got to Magee. Since it was time for evening worship at that point in our trip, Linda took us to the Magee Methodist Church. "Isn't this something," I was thinking to myself as we stopped and got out. Then, even more surprisingly, I heard my name called. Charlie Schultz, who had recently served my home church, had been appointed to Magee, and his son, Buster, was sitting on the church steps when we drove up. I introduced Linda to Buster, and as we began to make our way into the sanctuary, I didn't even try to keep a smile off my face. "Why should I," I thought, "I have the wife I want, and the first thing we're doing as a married couple is attending church."

The manager of the Highway Host Motel in Hattiesburg, William DeLoach, a friend of Daddy's, got Linda and me a complimentary room at his Jackson motel as his wedding gift to us. Perhaps it wasn't the motel's honeymoon suite, but it felt like it to me. The room was spacious, well appointed, and, best of all, cool. Linda's car wasn't air conditioned and August 16 had been as hot as every other day that month.

To show Linda she hadn't married a slouch, I insisted she relax while I unloaded the car. Absentmindedly, however, I forgot to unlock the motel door when I departed. Finding my entry blocked as I stood, suitcases in hand, a few moments later, I decided to amuse Linda by knocking on the door as if I was a visitor. She played along with my silliness and, upon hearing the knock, asked who was there. "Fuller Brush man," I replied. Hearing that announcement, she flung open the door with mock enthusiasm and invited me in.

Before we went to bed that night, Linda insisted we kneel and have a prayer. I complied, of course, and, in my prayer, I gave solemn thanks for the opportunity to live out the rest of my life with the woman I loved.

The next day, we boarded the train as scheduled and headed for St. Louis, Missouri, a city neither of us had ever visited, but one that we felt would be an interesting place for a honeymoon. In my case, I was also excited about being in the home state of President Harry S. Truman. He had proven that a man of mostly ordinary abilities could, in many ways, make an extraordinary president. Knowing I too was quite ordinary in most ways, I wanted to be a little like him and accomplish more than might be expected.

Somewhat foolishly, it seems to me now, I didn't make Linda and me a hotel reservation in St. Louis. I reasoned that a city of that size would have plenty room vacancies from which we might choose once we got there. My reasoning was sound up to a point, but what I didn't anticipate was that our visit might coincide with that of a large number of conventioneers, but it did. As it happened, a very large number of black Shriners had converged on the city, and they had gotten there somewhat earlier than Linda and I had, a fact we quickly discovered.

As Linda and I collected our suitcases and told the driver at the cabstand we'd like to be taken to a hotel where we could get a room, we sensed some hesitation on his part. He did say, however, he'd do his best. As he got under the wheel and pulled away from the curb, he looked around at us and said, "I'm not exactly sure where to take you, but I'm going to try the Chase Park Plaza."

With the luck of the Irish, though Linda and I both are of Scottish ancestry, the Chase did have a vacancy, and we happily took it even though the rate was high - $24, as a matter of fact. It is often true, however, that you get what you pay for, and I can say without any hesitation the Chase was nice. Had it not been for our limited budget, we would have stayed there for all of our four-day honeymoon, but, instead, we elected to move a couple of blocks over to a much more reasonably priced Forest Park Hotel for our last two days.

Choosing to make no specific agenda, Linda and I just spent our time together doing whatever struck us at the moment. We walked around various parts of the city and visited several of its famous sites, including the great arch marking the passage to the west, which was well under construction at the time. We also visited the renowned Famous-Barr, where I bought a book about all of our nation's presidents. Famous-Barr seemed to me to be a strange name for a store, but it was an elegant facility.

Pretending they had come to town just for our benefit, Linda and I went to the Shriners parade along with a few hundred thousand other folk and enjoyed their music and the precision of their marchers. It was unlike anything we'd ever done before, and we both got a real kick out of the experience.

On our way back to Mississippi that weekend, our train was carrying a number of Shriners back to their homes as well. Upon seeing us, especially me, wearing my shades and carrying my cane, a couple of them said, "If you need anything, just call for Chip or Brock. We'll be glad to help you any way we can." There was a slight smell of alcohol in the air as they spoke, but I could tell their offer was sincere, and I would certainly have called for them had the need arisen. Sometimes you can just tell when you can count on a person, even a total stranger.

When we left the train in Jackson, we decided to visit with Daddy, Lucille, Sue and Ann for a couple of days before going to Hattiesburg to get everything ready for the beginning of the school year. It was a relaxed time for us and a good opportunity for us to get our second wind before our lives would become much more active. We stayed in my old room, and I could not keep from remembering many of the thoughts and feelings I had entertained only a little over four years earlier. In my wildest dreams during that awful period of my life, I couldn't have imagined how much better off I would be in such a brief period. Boy, was I glad to be alive.

Not much over a week later, if anything, I was even more enthusiastic about the way my life was going. By then, Linda and I had moved into a one-bedroom apartment in USM's married student facility called Pine Haven. Faculty members were permitted to live there if student demand was low and space was available. And, thank goodness, it was. By one of those strange coincidences of life, our next door neighbors, Mel and Cara Lee Jones, were good friends of ours from previous years at USM. They helped us to get off to a good start in Pine Haven, and we, ultimately, had three happy years in our little home bearing the designation "E204" of Pine Haven.

During our time at Pine Haven, we also had the pleasure of acquiring the friendship of David and Nancy Culp, a friendship which, like that of Mel and Cara Lee Jones, was to stand the test of time. Regretfully, Dave died over a decade ago, but Nancy still survives, along with their children, Jennifer and Dave, the namesake of his dad.

As would obviously be the case, many things occurred in our lives during the Pine Haven period, but, thankfully, many of them were either happy experiences from the outset or eventually turned out well. Linda Jean married the love of her life, Charles Carruth, with whom she would eventually have five children, giving each a name beginning with the letter "K." In turn, they were Kevin, Keith, Kyle, Kreg and Kandace. Later, they would add an "R" when Robyn Woodward joined the family.

With Linda's sisters, Margaret and Becky, still living in the family home in New Augusta, only 20 miles away, we regularly had the pleasure of their company. Linda's parents always made us feel welcome when we visited them, especially on the weekends, and, as a consequence, we did it often.

My sister Sue had the awful experience of being struck by a car when she was only fifteen. So many of her bones were broken, she had to be in a body cast for a month and a half, but remarkably, she came through the experience without a great deal of permanent damage. Linda and I visited her as often as we could and tried to be of some help, especially while she was still in her cast. Trouper that she was, Sue continued her school work as she recuperated and, as was shown a few years later when she graduated as the valedictorian of her class, never skipped a beat.

During the first year of our marriage, Linda taught at New Augusta. That was her first job offer when she left Pascagoula, so she decided to hedge her bets and take it. Contrary to what might be expected, teaching in the school where she had been a student only a few years before turned out to be a good experience for her, and, had it not been for the fact she had to drive twenty miles to get to work, she might well have been content to stay where she was. As it happened, however, Hattiesburg offered her a position, and she elected to make her life a little simpler by taking it. That decision proved to be a good one, and things went well for her during both the school year of '65-'66 and that of '66-'67.

Being a college instructor worked out well for me, all things considered, and my initial three years in the profession got me off to a good start. Among other things, however, I learned that conducting class all by yourself for a full period required the mastery of a tremendous amount of material. I could hardly believe how much preparation was required to assure I could get through each class without having egg on my face. Fortunately, I always had the benefit of a student assistant to help me in making my preparations. One of them, Jimmy Williamson, was brilliant, and he proved to be absolutely invaluable to me. With life taking the strange turns it sometimes does, years later I was able to partially repay him by helping him to land an excellent position with Mississippi's Research and Development Center. As it happened, he held that job his entire working life, dying all too young in 1991, a victim of AIDS.

As a former student of my colleagues, Dr. Wilber and Dr. Hatcher, I had excellent role models, so I tried to be as much like them as I could. For the most part, my students seemed to like me well enough, and I only felt I was cheating them somewhat when I had to cover topics that I had failed to master as well as I would have liked.

Linda Jean and Charles were still in school during my first year as an instructor, and although all of us were too busy to permit regular visits, we did get to spend some time together, and I've always felt I was lucky to have such a benefit. Perhaps, partly because of those visits, Linda Jean asked me to give her away when she and Charles married at the end of the summer of '65. Though I was honored to perform that function, I regretted very deeply the circumstances giving rise to it. It would have been much better if our Daddy could have had appropriately discharged those responsibilities. In Linda Jean's mind, however, the man she call Daddy had not performed very well in that role.

Throughout this period, however, my relationship with Daddy continually improved. Linda and I drove up to Jackson fairly often to visit with him and Lucille and, of course, Sue and Ann. All four of them made us feel very welcome and being with them was invariably a treat. I had to set aside any guilt feelings I might have had that somehow by having a good relationship with this part of my family, I was being disloyal to Mama. I was trying to make the best out of the situation, and I could only hope everyone involved would understand.

Being practical, there was another very good reason for me to visit in Jackson, especially as 1967 approached. I was making plans to realize my childhood dream of being in politics, and Daddy was an integral part of that plan. Like me, he believed if I could get myself elected to the legislature, a number of doors would open for me that otherwise might well remain shut.

Chapter 10

Running for the House of Representatives

In the early spring of 1967 I made one of the most important and, ultimately, one of the most gratifying decisions of my entire life. I decided to run for the Legislature.

In a sense, in was almost inevitable that I would enter politics. My people on both sides of my family had held public office or assumed important public responsibilities for generations. In fact, on my father's side of the family, one of my grandfathers, several times removed, Benjamin Huff, was a delegate to the Mississippi Constitutional Convention of 1817, and as such helped to usher Mississippi into statehood. Two other Huff forebears, Newton Lawrence and Adolphus, were elected to the Mississippi House of Representatives in the middle 1800s and the early 1900s. Then in 1939, my father, who was one-half Huff, was elected to his first of two terms as Amite County's Superintendent of Education.

On my mother's side, James Ambrose Parker, another grandfather several times removed, served as Amite County's treasurer for 12 years just prior to Mississippi's Centennial Celebration. Not many years later, my great-uncle, John H. Parker, became a very public person and, among other positions, was Chancery Clerk of Amite County. Remarkably T. P. Herndon, his nephew and my cousin, was able to succeed him in that position.

At the time I entered politics, no one in my family on either side was holding public office. Beyond any question, that was to my advantage. As it happened, however, an uncle of mine, George Robertson, decided to enter the race for County Superintendent against Annie Andrews, who had succeed Daddy in that office. Uncle George and I both knew the dangers inherent in having two Robertsons on the same ballot, so we very carefully avoided significant contact with one another throughout our campaigns.

Of the many problems I faced early on, the most perplexing was that of deciding which seat in the House I would seek. There were two posts designated as one and two, and I had to decide between them. In each instance, I would be running in Amite, Franklin, and Wilkinson Counties, but the post I chose to seek would determine against whom I would be running. Therein lay the problem, because early on there was no way to know who would seek what. It was commonly known that Frank Wall, who was currently serving only Amite County, would be seeking reelection, and I knew I didn't want to run against him, but I didn't know which post he would choose. It was also generally accepted that Walker Carney was going to run, but no one knew which post he would choose either. Both for political and personal reasons, I didn't want him to be my opponent. He was well known in all three counties, and his sister was married to Barney Poole, a brother of my aunt, Willodene Robertson.

Two other men were also expected to run. They were Douglas Leonard, an ag. man from Franklin County, and Homer Smith, a former supervisor from Amite county. As with Frank and Walker, there was no way to tell which post each of them would choose.

Various supporters of mine encouraged me to make my decision early, but I kept hoping something would happen that would give me a sense of direction. By mid spring, however, with the Democratic primary being only a few months away, I decided to simply follow the dictates of my heart. It told me that I could not run against Frank Wall, because at a time when I needed his help to get a job, he did everything he possibly could for me. As a result, I decided to seek post two, which would leave Frank free to choose post one, if that's what he wanted to do.

Soon after I announced, Walker made his decision, and to my deep regret, he decided to run against me. When Daddy learned what had happened, his level of regret was even greater than mine. He never said so, but I suspect he feared we couldn't beat Walker. To some extent, I had that fear myself, but I still felt I had done the right thing.

A few days later I learned that in addition to having Walker as an opponent, I would also have Douglas, but that news wasn't upsetting. Intuitively, I knew that having a third man in the race wasn't all bad. Far from it. It would mean, almost beyond question, that there would have to be a second primary which, I felt, would enhance my chances of ultimate victory. With three of us being pitted against one another in the first primary, Walker almost surely couldn't win the race outright. To do so would require him to get more votes than Douglas and me combined. I didn't believe he could do that, and if I was right, I'd have three additional weeks to gain support and, hopefully, be the number one candidate in the second primary.

Though Walker J., as he was often called, had the advantage of being better known than I, he had one serious limitation when being compared with me. I had Linda and he didn't. Regardless of what he did, he couldn't change the reality that I had a wife and he was single. The fact that she was pretty and also willing to work as hard as I was just made things that much better. To keep the record straight, however, it must be kept in mind that not one time did I ever say to anyone that it should be noted I was a married man and Walker J. wasn't, but of course I didn't have to. Everywhere I went, Linda was there and, consciously or subconsciously, it was bound to register with people.

From the outset Linda and I had one main strategy. Every day, we got out and campaigned and saw as many people as we possibly could. There were countless sub strategies, such as never passing a country store without stopping and once there, never leaving without buying something, but mostly we just got out there and worked at seeing the people. A friend of mine from Hattiesburg who was a member of the Senate at the time, Ed Pittman, recommended I get an aerial map of each county, and I did so early on. The maps were unbelievably accurate and they contained enough information to enable Linda and me to keep ourselves constantly oriented. We knew, day by day, what we had done, and as importantly, what was left to do. Every house on every road was designated, and we kept a red pencil that we used to mark our progress. Not once did we get lost, and we never were confused about where we left off in our house-to-house canvas. As a consequence, I often was able to impress people whom I met by letting them know when they could expect to see me. I recall, for instance, a rally in Franklin County, at which a man came up to me and said that although I had gone to see all his neighbors, but not him, he was still going to vote for me. Immediately, I asked him where he lived and when he told me, I informed him with all the sincerity I could muster that the only reason I hadn't been to his house yet was that I simply hadn't gotten that far up his road. Then I assured him I would be there very soon and would be looking forward to seeing him. He left with a smile on his face, but I guarantee it wasn't any bigger than mine. I knew I not only had confirmed his support but that he would be telling people far and wide that his friend, Jimmy, surely did know how to make a campaign for public office.

Typically, when Linda and I stopped at a house, we would both go up and greet whomever was at home. I would introduce the two of us and, after handing over one of my campaign cards, I would give my spiel. It always contained a little personal information about me and a request at the end for the listener's vote and support. If I got a favorable response, I would always take the next step and ask for all the help that could possibly be managed. If I didn't get a favorable response, I would still say something friendly and congenial. In any case, however, I didn't linger long. Saying too much can get you into trouble, especially in politics.

On at least one occasion, though, I did violate my own rule. It happened because a man in Franklin County upon whom I had called took it upon himself to tell me that he couldn't support me because my opponent was a much better man than I. The more I listened to him, the more I knew I wasn't going to stand still for it. When he finished, I said, "Well, you can just go ahead and vote for my opponent, because I made arrangements to win without your support." I smiled a little as I said those words to him, but he and I both knew it wasn't much of a joke. Saying what I did probably didn't serve me well from some standpoints, but I just couldn't bring myself to let him get away with what he had said. When I left him, all I could do was hope what I had told him would ultimately be proven true.

Fortunately, I did have a little evidence by then to support a fairly high level of confidence. For various reasons, my campaign was going quite well, especially in Franklin County. For the most part, the people there received Linda and me virtually with open arms. I started out knowing very few people in the county, but my aunt, Maude Cothren, was both well known and well liked. Moreover, her son, James Arthur, and stepsons, Wallace, A. J., and Ottis, also had broad connections. A. J., especially, liked me extremely well and was willing to brag on me every chance he got.

In addition, I had made several friends from Franklin County as a result of my teaching. Donald Cotten, for example, a former student of mine who had both friends and substantial family connections was a very active supporter. Also, largely through him, I had gained the friendship of David Campbell who had a great love for politics. Although he was only 19 and couldn't even vote, he proved to be an excellent strategist and served, unofficially, as my Franklin County campaign manager. Remarkably, his youth seemed to redound to my advantage.

From the very outset in Franklin County, I had also enjoyed the full support of Mr. Cliff Herring. His political savvy was second to none, and his advice was always sound. Through him I gained the support of several large families and their connections as well. Few things are better for a candidate than having a well-established political leader promoting him at every turn.

Daddy functioned both as my overall campaign advisor and as the director of my campaign in Wilkinson County along with my uncles, Timer and Dago Robertson, as they were called, and my cousin, Billy Berryhill. Since I didn't have much of a power base in Wilkinson County, I needed their help very badly.

Though the impact of the voting rights act of 1965 would be substantial throughout my entire district, in Wilkinson County it would be critical. Making inroads among those new voters without alienating the old voters would require a great deal of finesse, but Daddy seemed equal to the task, especially with a little help along the way. Linda and I campaigned there some, of course, but never to the same extent as in Amite and Franklin.

In politics as in life generally, you use what you have. In my case what I had was family connections second to none. In Amite County, especially, that was to prove to be a decisive factor. Mama had made her home there practically all of her 61 years, and virtually no one was more highly regarded than she. Though she had no real affinity for politics, the fact that her son was seeking office was enough to assure she would help every way she could. Among many other contributions she made to my race, she and I conducted a door-to-door canvas of Liberty, taking up several of her Thursday afternoons, the only time she had off Monday through Saturday, in the process.

Like Mama, Barbara Ann didn't care much for politics, but she too was willing to do what she could. The fact she was married to a Payne also served me well. Like ours, the Payne family had a long history in the county. Together, Barbara Ann and her husband, Robert, would be able to influence a substantial number of voters.

Though Maureen was in Jackson, she still had friends in the county from her school days, and she too was able to exert some influence. Her husband, Bill, as always, did what he could, including providing some financial support.

For various reasons, my sister Linda Jean and her husband, Charles Carruth, were willing and able to spend quite a bit of their time actively campaigning for me. Their presence was seen in various parts of the county throughout my race, but they concentrated their efforts especially in the Eastfork and Gillsburg communities where they felt they could have the greatest impact. Both of them had large numbers of friends on whom they could count, and as the son of Hubert and Inez Middleton Carruth, Charles had scores of relatives.

Linda and Charles also proved to be creative campaigners. For example, they generated quite a bit of interest and, no doubt, quite a bit of support as well by using a sound system on their car to advertise my candidacy far and wide. Linda Jean drove, smiling and nodding to all she saw as Charles used the microphone with the attached loudspeaker to tell all who heard what a lovely fellow I was and why I ought to be elected to the House. I had the pleasure of seeing them in action when they came through Liberty, and as would be expected, they made quite an impression. Linda Jean wasn't the only one smiling as a result.

On another occasion when a rally was held in Liberty, Linda Jean donned a straw hat to which she had attached numbers of my campaign cards of varying colors and made a point to speak to every person present. My nephew, Bobby, Barbara and Robert's oldest son, thought the idea was so cute that he wanted to wear the hat for a while. Being gracious and, as a teacher, knowing how important such a thing can be to a child, Linda Jean consented and Bobby had himself a nice time walking around showing off his hat. I noticed, on that occasion, his smile was broad and not the least bit shy.

Working always at least ten hours a day, Linda and I covered every nook and cranny of Amite and Franklin Counties and much of Wilkinson County. Virtually the only break from that routine Linda got was when Mama and I covered Liberty. No doubt her face would hurt from all that smiling, but she kept at it day after day just as I did.

In one instance, I was surprised to find that Linda could also be quite aggressive. By chance we called on a young man in Franklin County whom she had known several years before when he lived in New Augusta. I gave him my usual spiel, and when I finished, she wasn't pleased with his noncommittal response and immediately gave him to understand that she expected his full support. I stood back and listened with my mouth a little agape as she told him how the cow ate the cabbage. She finally had to relent somewhat, however, because as he explained, my opponent, Douglas Leonard, was one of his relatives. We did, however, succeed in getting the enthusiastic support of his mother. Well, I thought as we headed back to the car, we didn't make a clean sweep of this household, but Walker J. didn't get anything, and there's not much time left.

A couple of weeks later when the first primary was held, the outcome was largely as I had predicted. Though Walker J. led the ticket, he didn't get the required majority for outright victory. I was mildly disappointed in my vote, but mostly I was just determined to do better in the second or runoff primary.

Unlike Walker J., I had no job responsibilities to distract me and I was pretty sure I wanted to win more than he did. As a result, I worked harder than ever in those last three weeks of August, and I could tell my efforts were paying off.

The weather certainly didn't cooperate though. We didn't get a drop of rain and the temperature soared. Every day when Linda and I came in from campaigning, we were coated with dust and grime, but we never let up. We were constantly on the move making as many stops as possible and shaking as many hands as we could. I believe, beyond any question, it was that extra effort that ultimately turned the tide.

The day of the second primary proved to be one of the most exciting and gratifying days of my life. Watching the vote totals change as ballot box after ballot box came in, gave me a thrill unlike anything I'd ever known. It took a good while for the trend to be established as my family and I monitored everything from Mama's home on election night, but it finally did happen.

Daddy let Sue stay up and watch the returns come in, giving her a thrill she never forgot, but Ann was too young to stay up that late. Sometime well after ten, Daddy figured he'd better go to his in-laws, Julius and CBelle Dawson, to check on Ann and, to his surprise, found her awake. She immediately asked, "Has Jimmy won yet?" Giving her his usual smile and pat, he simply said, "Not yet."

Not long after that, however, the outcome seemed certain, and everybody in my family relaxed somewhat. You could see it in all of us, perhaps especially Linda Jean and Charles. When the ballot boxes came in where they had concentrated their efforts, they could hardly have been more pleased.

Many other people, of course, had helped to assure my victory, and I was intensely proud of the confidence they had shown in me. As a result I was thinking of them when my childhood friend Joe Gordon walked across the street from the courthouse to Mama's so he could congratulate me. I appreciated his thoughtfulness, and I told him so, but I also made it clear that I knew it was a team victory. Interestingly, that fact did not diminish my personal joy. In actuality, it was enhanced by it.

Another factor that contributed to the sweetness of victory was the gentlemanly way that Walker J. accepted defeat. He gave me a personal congratulatory call when the results were known and I could tell from his voice he bore me no ill will. Happily, I didn't feel badly toward him either. He had fought the good fight and, quite literally, had made the race too close for comfort. To his credit, he kept his campaign as clean as I kept mine, so from that standpoint, neither of us had any regrets.

After making a final round through all three of my counties, Linda and I took a few days off to get rested up and get accustomed to the idea of me being a member of the Mississippi House of Representatives. We went over to New Augusta and visited with her mom and dad and sisters, Margaret and Becky. They were proud of us, of course, and it was fun for Linda and me to be out from under the strain of the previous four months.

While in southeast Mississippi, we also went by to see our friend, Dr. McCain. That visit proved to be both enjoyable and beneficial. In addition to giving me his compliments on my victory, he did me the high honor of asking me to be a recruiter for the university during that fall. Sure, I thought as I assented to his request, helping kids figure out how they can go to college will be a great way for me to spend the next four months.

Chapter 11

Serving in the House

Shortly after the year got under way in 1968, I took the oath of office as a member of the Mississippi House of Representatives. Once again, I was beginning a chapter of my life very close to the date of my accident. As I raised my hand and swore that I would uphold the Constitution and laws of the United States and the Constitution and laws of the state of Mississippi, I was very conscious of how far I had come in only eight years. It also occurred to me, ironically, that in all likelihood if I had not had the accident, I would never have realized the dream of becoming a legislator.

Since there were 122 House and 52 Senate members taking office at the same time, the Capitol was overflowing with people. There were family members and various other well-wishers from throughout the state with quite a few of them being present in deference to me. Sadly, the one who would have enjoyed it the most, my daddy, was absent. He had died less than a month and a half earlier, but I did not allow myself to dwell on that loss. I made sure my inauguration day was a happy time for Linda and me and our families.

It was also an historic occasion. For the first time since reconstruction, a black man would be occupying a seat in the legislature. Like the integration of The University of Mississippi, which had occurred a bare five and a half years earlier, albeit by force, this was a change of monumental proportions. As a consequence, national attention was again focused on Mississippi. That time, thank goodness, the publicity took on a much more positive character.

The one on whom all the attention was centered was Robert Clark from Holmes County, and he did an unexpected thing. Very deliberately, he assured that every House member present that day would wind up on national TV. He did that by entering the House on the Speaker's right and then walking all the way around the entire chamber before finally claiming his seat only a few feet from the door he had entered. Cameras followed every step he made and, thus, all of us were captured by them. A friend of mine from California wrote to let me know she had seen me on the evening news.

With Robert and me both being college teachers and having other things in common, we soon became friends and that friendship would prove to be durable. He was everything his constituents, and the rest of us for that matter, could have wanted, and I felt honored to have served with him.

Shortly after the session got under way, we went through the formality of electing Johnny Junkin of Adams County as our Speaker. He was a highly regarded member of the House and a very capable legislator but a very conservative one. When he made his committee appointments, he also showed himself to have a good memory of those who had not given him their full support. Contrary to my wishes, the only appointment I got that was of real interest to me was the Education Committee. I would have liked to have served on Colleges and Universities, but that privilege was denied me.

Though the Mississippi House of Representatives is very similar to its model, the U. S. House, the two differ in at least one important regard. In the Mississippi House, especially at that time, the role of political parties was essentially nonexistent. Virtually everyone was elected as a Democrat, and therefore reference to party membership never occurred. When key decisions were made, the outcome was determined by various factors, but party was not one of them.

Largely because of the very limited role played by party, seniority wasn't an absolute prerequisite in determining who would go into positions of power. Even so, most members were expected to serve a term or two before they could expect to play a dominant role in House affairs. Once in a while a junior member would not have to wait his or her turn to rise in the hierarchy, but it didn't happen often.

Another factor of great importance in determining who would and who would not have power was geography. To state it bluntly, if you didn't come from north of Jackson, your chances of being a real force was severely limited. This was an unwritten rule, of course, but that didn't mean it wasn't real. On the surface, Johnny Junkin, a native of Natchez, who was still able to get himself elected Speaker, was an exception, but he met the other standards. In temperament and philosophy he was acceptable, so he could be forgiven for not coming from the right part of the state.

Contrary to usual practice, the man who was elected governor in 1967 gained his prominence through service on the national level not on the state level. His name was John Bell Williams and he was able to win the governor's race largely because he had been a member of the U. S. House for two decades. As was soon evident, however, his service in the Congress didn't prepare him well to be Mississippi's chief executive.

From the standpoint of constitutional power, the office of Mississippi's governor is relatively weak. Nonetheless, it has very substantial informal powers and the person holding the office is looked to by the legislature for leadership. If that leadership is provided, significant progress can be made. If it is not, the legislature will likely flounder and serious problems are almost inevitable.

In large measure, the latter is what occurred, especially in the early part of our first session. As a consequence, we wound up meeting for an extraordinarily long period of time. There are many implications of a long session, not the least of which is that it imposes a great burden on most members of the House and the Senate. Simply stated, the Legislature doesn't pay very well. Obviously then, the longer the session, the less time there is for members to make additional money from other sources.

Ultimately, the session proved to be fairly productive, but since it took us more than seven months to get our work done, no one felt that it had been a rousing success. Because of my legislative goals, however, I felt quite pleased at what we had accomplished. For example, we had made quite a bit of progress in public education, including granting a substantial increase in teachers' salaries.

We also passed legislation to assure that Mississippi would have a system of public broadcasting that, in many ways, would be second to none.

Feeling good about my service in the Legislature, however, paled in importance when compared to how I felt about my personal life. Ecstatic is the word that comes to mind to describe that sentiment. The principle reason for how I felt was that Linda became pregnant early in the session and our baby was due in the second week of October. Since Linda and I were the only couple in the entire House to be expecting a baby, we got a great deal of attention. With Linda having few obligations to prevent her from doing so, she spent a great deal of her time at the Capitol, and that made it possible for my colleagues to monitor the progress of her pregnancy. Many of them were quite forthright and, on seeing her from time to time, would give her careful scrutiny, and then remark to one another right there in her presence that she was beginning to show quite a bit. Though embarrassing to some degree, that type of attention was also pleasant in many ways and it added to our continuing and growing excitement. Even the Speaker, whom I scarcely knew, was pleased about Linda's pregnancy. I learned that rather remarkable fact one day in early May when I was asked to open the session with prayer. While sitting with the Speaker on the platform, in the few minutes prior to getting things under way, I told him that in October I was going to become a father. He responded immediately and enthusiastically by slapping me on the leg several times as he said, "Now you're living." He was certainly correct, but I was still quite surprised to hear him say such a thing.

With a baby on the way, Linda and I also decided '68 would be the year we would buy our first home. It was the little house owned by Bobby and Ann Kinabrew, which we had been renting since the late spring of 1967. Being on a street just east of the center of town, we felt its location was ideal. Initially the Kinabrews asked $5,000 for it, but finally agreed to sell for $4,800. Interestingly, our monthly payments wound up being slightly less than we had been paying in rent. We financed our purchase through FHA and wound up with a monthly obligation of $40.

Soon after we acquired ownership of our home, our friend, Carey

Reynolds, offered to paint it for us. At first, he completely rejected the idea of us paying him anything for his work, but we finally talked him into accepting $1 per hour. Even so, he must have seriously underestimated the number of hours he spent on the project because we wound up paying him only $40.

In addition to getting our home ready for our baby, we also bought a brand-new air-conditioned automobile. The little Rambler that Linda had bought in 1963 was fine for her, but we felt we needed a larger and more comfortable car when there would be three of us. Being of Scottish ancestry, I remember its exact cost. Including the tax, the total came to $3,191.

Fortunately, Linda and I did not have to survive solely on my income as a Representative. I was able to secure a teaching position at the new Natchez campus of USM and supplement my income between legislative sessions. By hiring a young friend to be my driver, I could commute to Natchez fairly easily each evening I had a class. Fellows such as Jimmy Ratcliff, Ronnie Reynolds, Hal Sterling, Joey Vigneault, and Sammy Walsh seemed quite happy to pick up a few dollars for being my chauffeur.

By the time the fall quarter began, Linda was only about six weeks away from her delivery date. Mama had agreed to drive us to the Centreville Hospital when the time came, and, as luck would have it, that time happened to be at the inconvenient hour of 1 a.m. Having had the experience of delivering four babies herself, Mama knew it would take Linda a good while to actually become a mother, so she got us checked in and then went home to catch a nap before getting her workday under way at the M & T Store.

Linda was assigned a nice, comfortable room in which I was permitted to stay as well. Throughout the early morning hours, she was reasonably comfortable, and I tried to be a pleasant companion for her. Occasionally, I would doze off as I ran out of things to say, but, for the most part, I helped her to pass the time fairly well until daylight.

The hospital staff was kind enough to bring me breakfast at 7:00, but my stomach was too nervous for me to derive my usual enjoyment from my favorite meal. Since Linda was in labor, she was denied the privilege of eating breakfast, which was probably just as well. Even in its early stages, labor prevents a woman from having any interest in food.

After taking her kids to school, Barbara Ann came down and spent the day with us. She was a source of great comfort to me, but, as the day wore on and Linda's pain became more and more acute, nothing seemed to provide her any distraction. That was a matter of great concern, both to Barbara and to me, but we were helpless to do anything about it. On more than one occasion, Barbara Ann spoke to the nurses about giving Linda some help, but they never were able to rise to the occasion. Linda's physician, my cousin Dr. James Poole, "Sonny Boy," as he was called by those of us who knew him well, came in to see her with increasing frequency as the day wore on, but he, too, was unable to do anything to reduce Linda's pain. By mid afternoon, when Barbara had to leave to pick up her children from school, her nerves were worn to a frazzle. Looking into Linda's brown eyes, full of pain hour after hour, as Barbara had done, had taken a toll.

For the next two hours, the nurses and Dr. Poole came and went every few minutes, it seemed, as I became more and more agitated. Linda did not cry out in her pain, but I knew it was constant and, often, excruciating. On more than one occasion, she told me that she didn't think she could stand it. In desperation, I tried to provide some relief by telling her my best jokes. To her credit, she was patient with me in my efforts, but she did not find my humor to be the least bit helpful.

Finally, at 5:00 p.m., Dr. Poole came in and told me to accompany a nurse down to the expectant fathers' waiting room. After I left, Linda was taken to delivery and I knew the ordeal was just about over. I had every confidence in Sonny Boy, but I still felt more than a little apprehensive as the minutes dragged by. I said a little prayer of thanksgiving and waited, my hands clasped together and held between my knees, perhaps to keep them from shaking.

At 5:30 p.m., a nurse came and told me everything was fine as she escorted me back to Linda's room. Unbeknownst to me, a few minutes later, another nurse, acting contrary to Dr. Poole's instructions that the baby be placed on the bed beside her mother, carried her down the hall for all to see as she brought her toward a greatly relieved young father. As Linda was being brought into her room, our baby was placed in my arms, and I had the high honor of being able to hold her first. Her delivery had been described as normal, but that was an obvious mistake. There was nothing normal about what had happened. All of it was marvelous, even miraculous. As if I knew what I was doing, I cradled the baby in my arms and called her by name. I said, "Hello, Margaret Estell. I'm your daddy. Welcome to the world." Tears filled my eyes as I spoke, but they had been caused by a sense of wonder. What I felt was unlike anything I had ever known. A heavenly choir should have been singing the "Hallelujah Chorus."

Linda watched me from her bed and after what she felt was a sufficiently long time for her to wait, she called my name and asked me to bring our baby to her. When I laid Margaret Estell in Linda's arms, I leaned over and put a kiss on Linda's forehead. It was my plan to deliver the speech I had carefully rehearsed in my head. I was going to tell her how proud I was of her and what a great Mom I knew she would be. Then I was going to say that we would continue to have a good life together because of the lovely person she was. These things and others were going to be said by me in such a manner as to leave no doubt about my sincerity and the depth of my feelings. What actually happened, however, was that my emotions completely got the best of me, and my speech was cut short. In fact, it consisted of three words. I said, "Linda, I am," and that was as far as I could go. Several times I tried to get myself under control, but it was hopeless. Finally, I gave in and laid my head against Linda's shoulder and let the tears flow. She seemed to understand what my good intentions were because she patted on me and said consoling words as I stood there and poured out my heart in the only way I could at the time.

When I regained my composure, Linda and I marveled together over the perfection of our daughter. All too soon, however, a nurse came in and took Margaret Estell to the nursery. Even though we knew we would have her back soon thereafter, it was still difficult for us to give her up.

Half an hour later, Mama, Barbara, Linda Jean, and Charles all came in together to see Margaret Estell for the first time. By then, I was feeling a little more normal, but I still couldn't hold back the tears as everybody talked about how pretty my daughter was and how well Linda had done throughout the entire experience.

Mama, Linda Jean, and Charles were not able to return until the next evening because of their work obligations, but Barbara joined us that morning and spent most of the day. Linda was still quite weak but feeling much better after a night's rest. Relatively speaking, I was in good form.

By a happy coincidence, my colleague from the Senate, John William Powell and his wife, Martha, were at the hospital as well, enjoying the birth of their first child – a son, whom they named John Wesley. We all agreed it was a rare privilege for us to be able to share with one another the great joy we were all feeling. All of us also got a kick out of listening to the staff talking about how extraordinary it was for two of their legislators to have their first child at virtually the same time.

On Saturday, we not only had a number of my family members to visit, but we also had the pleasure of a visit from much of Linda's family. Her mom, dad, sister Becky, brother-in-law Bobby, and a six-month-old niece Teresa arrived just before noon and stayed until 3:00. Linda's other sister, Margaret, was delayed in seeing her new niece for a period of time because of work responsibilities.

The following Monday, my cousin, Sherry Robertson, took me home so I could put new, blue sheets on the bed Linda and I would share as new parents. That was the only thing left to do. Margaret Estell's room had been made ready weeks before.

Barbara Ann drove our little family home the next day, with Linda holding Margaret Estell securely in her arms every foot of the way. I would have been glad to help, but my services were not needed. After dropping us off and helping us to get settled, Barbara went to town to pick up a few things for us. When she returned, she found Linda and me looking as if we knew what we were doing. Who knows, perhaps we did.

I had long since made the conscious decision that I was going to do everything for Margaret Estell that Linda did. My experience with babies wasn't very extensive but my desire to be a good father was not capable of being measured.

Of course I knew the basics of child care, and I was completely confident that I could learn the other things from those who were more expert.

Thanks to the generosity of Jimmy and Ivy Sharp, the parents of my childhood friend Jimmie Kathryn Sharp Simmons, Linda and I had recently bought a new washer and dryer at a very reasonable price. We knew we would put our purchases to good use, and that proved to be even truer than we could have imagined. I assumed the responsibility of washing, drying, and folding Margaret Estell's diapers and clothes, and, as I quickly found, those activities occurred regularly.

From the outset, I also did my share in changing Margaret Estell's diapers, including those that were more than simply wet. Happily, I found it to be a chore I didn't mind at all. In fact, I made up a little song that I sang as I worked.

My favorite job as a parent, however, was that of feeding the baby; holding her as she sucked contentedly on her bottle created a feeling of warmth. That feeling was enhanced each time I put her on my shoulder and snuggled her against my neck as I patted her back until a loud burp signaled the fact she had gotten the relief she needed. To satisfy my curiosity, I always counted the number of pats required to get the necessary result. Occasionally, the number would go as high as 200.

From the beginning, I was never separated from my daughter for more than a few hours at the time. Typically, I was at home with her every day and every night. Even when I had to go to Jackson, both she and Linda were able to accompany me. With the Legislature meeting on a biennial basis during the first half of my term, the only time I had to be in Jackson after the session of '68 was for a couple of weeks in the summer of '69. Several of the Great Society measures passed by the Congress under the leadership of President Johnson required state legislative action for their implementation, and Governor Williams called a special legislative session for that purpose. The most important of these programs were Medicaid and HeadStart. Both were somewhat controversial but the matching formula was so attractive, opposition was difficult to muster.

Major legislative duties did not occur again until the regular session of

1970. A recently adopted constitutional amendment would assure it would last only a few months, but I still wanted Linda and Margaret Estell to be with me if it could be managed. When Lucille learned of our need for housing, she graciously offered to rent us an apartment in her home. Naturally we took advantage of her generosity.

Contrary to any reasonable expectations (due to my short tenure), I wound up playing a leadership role on behalf of public education that year. In previous sessions, numbers of others had played that role, but 1970 was a very different time. In that session, many of the leaders of the past turned their backs on education. A recent U.S. Supreme Court decision was causing quite a stir because in it the Court announced the end of segregation. Almost overnight in the Legislature and within the state, generally, support for the public schools was seriously eroded. It was immediately apparent that many of the people who had been counted on in the past were going to fall by the wayside.

To my consternation, even the Chairman of the House Education Committee refused to assume the responsibility his position would seem to require. Contrary to usual practice, for example, he wouldn't be the author of the Minimum Foundation Education Bill, as it was typically called. In fact, to my complete disbelief, no member of longstanding on the Education Committee expressed any interest in being the bill's author. When this unwelcome information was made patently obvious to me, I had no alternative but to step forward. To the apparent chagrin of several committee members, I announced I would be the bill's principle author.

At the conclusion of the meeting, Lonnie Smith, a very capable Legislator from Pearl River County, informed me he would be a co-author, but he cautioned me to not introduce the bill until we had gotten the signature of at least half of our committee. I saw the clear wisdom of his advice, and I carried the bill around in my pocket for many days, buttonholing committee members as I could find them. To my immense relief, I eventually succeeded in getting the requisite number of names to assure the bill would come out of committee.

Though far from easy, we managed to provide public education enough support with our bill to assure its continuing viability. All votes in the House to determine the final outcome of a bill, are roll-call votes. Because of that fact, most members had no choice but to vote, "Aye." They knew they would have to face their constituents and explain their actions if they didn't do the right thing.

My support of public education caused me some problems, but most of my constituents understood my motivation. Only a few were hostile toward me as I traveled throughout the district. It was obvious I could expect to win reelection if I chose to run again. The weekly newspaper articles I began writing at the beginning of my term were deeply appreciated by virtually everyone and, of course, they not only kept the people informed, they provided me with constant free publicity.

As the time for me to announce my intentions with respect to further service drew nigh, I began to find many reasons why I shouldn't make another race. Quite unselfishly, I thought, Linda said she would go along with me regardless of what I decided. In the end, I couldn't justify running again, largely because of my long-range future. No one in his right mind would assume he could stay in politics indefinitely. That being so, I felt I had no alternative but to return to Hattiesburg and resume the life of an academician.

Despite the fact that I knew it was the best thing for my family, moving away from Amite County was a difficult thing to do. It meant leaving behind most of the people who loved me. Visiting them from time to time would be a poor substitute for being a regular part of their lives. Leaving also meant I would be giving up activities which meant a great deal to me, such as attending services in my home church every Sunday, going to town and hearing my name called by every person I met and being with friends such as James and Toots Stevenson who accepted me just exactly as I was.

With the emotional reservations I had about moving, I wasn't at all surprised by the lump in my throat which appeared the afternoon of August 13 when Linda's brother-in-law, Bobby Brewer, pulled up in front of our house in a U-Haul trailer large enough to take all our belongings to Hattiesburg. Her sister, Becky, came, too, so there would be a driver for both our cars.

Four hours later as Bobby and I rode along in a heavily laden U-Haul, reminiscing about things we had done in the past and talking about what we might do in the future, we would both have been very surprised had we known what lay ahead for us. Who could have predicted, for example, that eventually Bobby would become a United Methodist minister, and I would realize several goals I hadn't yet had the courage to even formulate?

Chapter 12

Reaching As High As Possible

When I got to Hattiesburg and began the fall Quarter at USM in a sense I was continuing a process that had begun much earlier.

Perhaps as early as the time Mr. Thume told me I should consider graduate work, I began to dream of earning a Ph.D. degree. It wasn't until I had launched my college teaching career, however, that I began to think seriously about setting a goal to realize that dream. As it was to happen, many years would have to pass and there would be three aborted attempts before I finally succeeded. Remarkably, however, virtually none of the courses I took, beginning in the summer of '65, proved to be wasted efforts. On the contrary, in 1976, when I finally settled on the idea of getting a Ph.D. in higher education from Ole Miss, the work I had done over the preceding eleven years had direct application.

Mainly because of its low cost and fairly easy accessibility, I chose LSU to be the school at which, in the summer of '65, I would take my first two doctoral-level courses-- political theory and constitutional law. After several visits to Baton Rouge and several long distance telephone calls, I got myself admitted and Linda and I were even able to find an on-campus couple who were going to be away and were, thus, happy to have us rent their apartment.

Both of my professors were pleasant and competent and my initial experience as a doctoral student turned out fine, all in all. The only serious difficulty I faced was that of getting all the reading done, but with the help of Linda and my sister, Sue, who came down and made recordings of much of my material, I was able to keep my head above water. It would have been ideal if the books I needed to read had already been recorded, but that wasn't the case. In fact, until many years after that, practically nothing I needed to read was available to me in audio.

It was also possible that summer to spend time with several of my old friends from Liberty who had relocated to Baton Rouge. Principle among them was my childhood friend, Dave Cupit. He and his wife took Linda and me both into their hearts and their home, and Dave even volunteered some of his time to read to me. By a happy coincidence, another friend from school days, James "Coot" Cain was in college at LSU after spending a four-year stint in the Air Force, and he and I had the pleasure of one another's company as well. Barbara Hays and Charles Paul Young were also in Baton Rouge at the time, and I got in an occasional visit with them as well.

Having made no better plan, Linda and I returned to LSU the following summer so I could take two additional courses. Luckily the same apartment was available, and once again we spent an enjoyable summer in Baton Rouge. That time I took a course in comparative federalism and a second theory course. I had no great interest in either of them, but I made sure I worked at them hard enough to make an acceptable grade.

As was the case the previous summer, Linda and I spent quite a little bit of time socializing. Among other enjoyable activities, we attended a gathering of several of my high school classmates, held on my initiative at the home of our friend, Frank Jones. Though it was hard for all of us to believe it could be so, by then we had been out of high school for nine years.

Politics took precedence over education in the following summer, and thereafter my life unfolded in a manner to make returning to LSU a virtual impossibility. Once I began my service in the legislature with part-time teaching on the side and full-time fatherhood, beginning in October of '68, there wasn't room for LSU or anything else.

Feeling the same enthusiasm I had experienced at LSU, I began my doctoral-level courses at USM as soon as the fall quarter got under way. I also resumed the same teaching schedule I had left in '67 and, so far as I knew, settled in for the long haul.

Taking two courses a quarter, I figured I could meet the course requirements for the doctorate in about two years. Earning a Ph.D. also required substantial work in two foreign languages, and I planned to get that process under way soon as well. There were other hurdles along the way, including especially the production of a dissertation. But I figured I'd meet them one by one.

Initially things went well and I felt good about my prospects. Dr. William Hatcher had become the departmental chairman, and he was doing an excellent job continuing the improvements begun earlier by Dr. Leon Wilber. My performance in class was typically rated more than acceptable and occasionally even superior. During the winter quarter of '72, I passed the doctoral qualifying examination and, from all appearances, was continuing on track.

There was, however, one thing that continually bothered me and I could not get it off my mind. Linda and I had made the decision we wanted to stay in Hattiesburg for the long haul, and that would mean I would need to have the necessary credentials to continue my employment at USM. If I earned my Ph.D. from there, I would seriously compromise my standing in the academic community. If, however, I earned my final degree elsewhere, my circumstances would be significantly improved.

With Tulane being in New Orleans and New Orleans being only a hundred miles from Hattiesburg, I decided it might be a viable alternative. A visit by Linda and me to Tulane in the early spring confirmed that belief, and I made arrangements to enter in the fall of '72.

If I could have driven myself to New Orleans, my life would have been a lot simpler, but since I couldn't I chose the only reasonable option that presented itself to me. I caught a bus that departed Hattiesburg at 4:00 a.m. and got me to New Orleans shortly after 6:00 a.m. From the bus station, it was fairly easy to catch a cab out to the university, and that was the pattern I adopted at the outset. To make things manageable, I chose only classes that met on Tuesday and Thursday mornings. At their conclusion, I could hustle back to the bus station in time to catch the 1:00 p.m. bus back home, if things went the way they were supposed to. After weeks of this, the dispatcher and I became friends, and he would always watch out for me. Sometimes he would even have to delay the bus's departure just for me. The other passengers might not have liked it, but he was taking care of his buddy, Jimmy.

Catching the bus so early in the morning was a nuisance, of course, so I was always trying to think of a better alternative. Eventually, I decided to advertise my needs in the *Hattiesburg American* newspaper. Remarkably, as a result of that publicity, I was able to find a man who commuted from Laurel to New Orleans each day because he didn't want to be away from home. His route took him through Hattiesburg, and he told me if I could follow his schedule, I could ride with him on a regular basis at no cost to me whatever. His name was Tommy Landrum, and he soon proved himself to be a completely reliable friend. For weeks on end he picked me up every Tuesday and Thursday morning at 5:00 a.m. at the intersection of 49 and 59 where his favorite gas station was located. By riding with him, I saved myself the cost of two bus tickets per week and had the pleasure of Tommy's company as well.

I attended Tulane for four semesters and as with both LSU and USM, the experience was generally pleasant and rewarding. Getting up at 2:30 a.m. in the morning that first year to catch a bus and a little later to catch Tommy wasn't the greatest thing in the world, but I had long ago concluded that in life, you do what you have to do.

All those trips back and forth to Tulane gave me the opportunity for a lot of introspection and to my dismay, I discovered I didn't really enjoy a lot of what I was required to do. The discipline of political science was changing fast and, despite my attempts to do so, I couldn't accommodate to those changes. I was making myself unhappy by trying to enjoy something I didn't find inherently interesting and I realized I had to do something about it. Life is too short to spend it doing what you don't want to do. The problem often times, however, lies in discovering what you do want to do. I wanted to settle that issue too, but since I couldn't, I dealt with the immediate problem by dropping out of Tulane at the end of the spring semester of '74.

Though I didn't come away with a degree, I did leave with a much better understanding of the American political system. More importantly, while there, I acquired a new friend for life. His name is Bernard Pyle and, since he is an incredibly bright person, had it not been for serious physical problems he undoubtedly would have earned his Ph.D. Instead, he was forced to return to Dallas, Texas. Soon thereafter, he began what was to be a distinguished career with the U. S. Postal Service.

Leaving Tulane caused quite a bit of self-doubt for me, but, happily I had other things that I could focus on. At almost exactly the time I finished my final course Linda, Margie, and I bought ourselves a brand-new home. With the help of several friends, especially H. J. and Orel Hedgepeth and sons Michael and Mitchell, we were able to get our things moved at virtually no cost. By H. J.'s own admission, his pickup truck was put to its best use ever.

Since moving to Hattiesburg in the late summer of 1971, Linda, Margie, and I had known only apartment living. Initially we were provided an apartment by our friends, Dottie and Mike Stetelman, and Ruth London, as payment for being resident managers of one of their complexes. When that job played out after a year and a half, another friend, Dan Ellis, gave us a nice price break on one of his apartments. In each instance, we were not uncomfortable, but having a home of our own was something we had been looking forward to for quite a while.

One of the main reasons for us wanting our own place was that we were about to expand the size of our family. In fact it was only two and one-half weeks from the day we moved until the birth of our second baby, a son.

Fortunately, Linda's time in labor wasn't nearly as long as her first experience. Her labor also began at a more convenient time. We didn't have to call our friend, Judy Cooper, until 7:00 a.m. to give us a ride to Forrest General Hospital. When Judy had made the kind offer to provide us with transportation, she had assured us she would be ready when needed, regardless of the hour, but I suspect she was as happy as I was that the hour turned out to be 7:00 a.m.

We were lucky in yet another way, too. Linda did not experience nearly as much intense pain the second time around. As before, I was with her every minute and I did everything I could think of to be of help. That time we didn't have Barbara Ann with us but, thank goodness, we didn't need her.

Shortly before Linda delivered our son, she was given medicine which significantly reduced the amount of pain she had been experiencing. As a result, the second time she gave birth was not nearly as painful as the first.

When the nurse came to Linda's room where I was waiting and announced that I was the father of a son, my heart swelled just as it had done when my daughter was born. That time, however, it was Linda who first held our new baby. I knew that was appropriate so when she made a point to have the nurse pass me by and hand our son to her, I only smiled and waited my turn.

As I held my son a few minutes later and talked to him, I again had the feeling that a holy thing had happened and I was completely in awe. Like his sister, he was perfect and as I had done when I held her, I cried tears of joy. Nothing else in the world can quite compare with holding your own newborn child.

As we had planned, we named our son James Arthur Robertson, III. I had been proud to be James Arthur Jr. and I wanted my son to have the name as well. What I couldn't decide, however, and neither could Linda, was exactly what we would call our son. I was considering calling him Arthur since that was the name my Daddy had used most of his life, but somehow I just wasn't completely sure that's what I wanted to do. The next day I learned that I wouldn't even have to think of it anymore. Margie settled the issue completely when she called the hospital and asked "How's James?" From that moment on, he was never called anything but James and though I have said the name thousands of times, in each instance I have said it with pride. Like his sister, he added a new dimension to my life and made it a great deal richer than I could have ever predicted.

On the morning of June 7th, when Linda and James came home from the hospital, Margie could not have been any more ready for them. She assured me she had done fine with her Maw Maw and Paw Paw McSwain in New Augusta, but it was obvious that she was anxious to be back with her mother and see her brother for the first time. In honor of the occasion, she was wearing her pink and white dress.

When they finally arrived, Margie rushed out to the car to greet them. After getting a much needed hug from her mother, she was able to put a kiss on the top of James' head. Then as Linda made her way into the house and back to our bedroom where everything was in readiness, Margie was with her step for step.

Immediately upon reaching our bedroom, Linda put James in his bassinet, and then with a sigh of relief, turned and got into her own bed. The instant she settled herself and looked back to check on James, she noted with considerable concern that he was not where she had put him. Instead of being in his bassinet, he was in the arms of his sister. Somehow, without Linda knowing what was happening, Margie had picked him up and was holding him as if he belonged to her. That began a very special relationship between the two of them. It has even become stronger over the years.

To my horror, the great joy I felt in having a son was almost extinguished less than a year following his birth. Just before the end of May of 1975, for no discernable reason, James became ill. Within twenty-four hours of the time he began to manifest various symptoms, he had to be hospitalized. Despite everything Linda and I tried to do, he seemed to be getting weaker and weaker. In fact, as I walked into Forrest General Hospital with James on my shoulder, his head sagged against my neck and his arms and legs hung limply against my chest.

After tests were run, James' pediatrician, Dr. George Herring, gave Linda and me the terrible news. With deep concern evident in his voice, he said, "Your son is very seriously ill. Somehow he has contracted a form of meningitis. I started him on some medicine that I hope will be effective, but this disease can be deadly." When I heard those words, fear like I had never known gripped both my body and my soul. I tried to keep from thinking that James might die but Dr. Herring had made it clear that outcome was not only possible, but might even be likely. I wasn't at all sure that my heart could stand the pain and I was in danger of throwing up right where I stood. Immediately I bowed my head and began praying as tears rolled down my cheeks. I prayed for James but mostly I prayed for strength and understanding. I knew that an ordeal lay before me and I had to get prepared for it.

After that I walked over and put my arms around Linda. Initially she had almost fainted, but by then she was able to stand and hug me. We stood like that for quite a while, holding one another in the pitiful hope that somehow things would work out right and James would survive.

The following three days were interminable. Linda and I stayed constantly by James' bedside, willing him to get well and trying to give him every assurance he could count on us. Doctors and nurses came and went as they gave James as much care as they could, but Linda and I were there continually. We touched him often so he would know of our presence and be able to sense our love. Perhaps I was foolish to believe what I was doing could make any difference because the meningitis had taken such a terrible toll that he was forced to simply lay in his bed and suffer. He never cried but that is probably because he lacked the strength to do so.

Finally, after the third day, the medicine seemed to be winning the fight with the meningitis. James became a little more responsive and from the small movements he was making we concluded some of his vigor was returning. Dr. Herring was guarded in his assessment of James' progress, but we could tell from his manner that there was reason for hope.

From the outset of James' illness, and in fact for the whole time he was in the hospital, our family and friends provided every support Linda and I could have wished. Even though they were sometimes required to don protective clothing they came to see us and several of them, including my stepmother, Lucille, stayed for hours. Without them I am not at all sure we could have made it.

By the sixth day there seemed to be little question that the worst was behind us. We still stayed with him every minute and he was still being administered intravenous medicine and nutrients, but we began to breathe more easily hour by hour.

In fact, I felt relaxed enough to leave the hospital long enough to spend some time with Margie. She had been staying with her grandparents in New Augusta and I had kept in touch by telephone but I felt she too needed some special attention.

On the third of June, Linda and I announced to the hospital staff that it was James' birthday. Without bothering to confer with us, they brought him his own special cake on a paper plate. To our immense relief, he was actually able to eat it. In fact, he could even partially feed himself. Feeling as if a great weight had been lifted from me, I leaned over and kissed James on the top of his head and said, "Buddy, would you like to give your ole Dad a bite of your cake?" He took his little hand, pinched off a morsel, and gave it to me. As I dropped it into my mouth, a tear rolled down my cheek before I could stop it, but I don't believe James saw it. If he did, perhaps he thought it was a tear of joy. If so, he was exactly right!

Two days later we were able to take James home. He was still quite weak, but the disease was gone from his body. We could only hope that no permanent damage had been done to him. In succeeding months and years, we were able to finally determine that was the case. In fact, the scars left by the shunts in his ankles are now the only evidence that James ever had anything wrong with him. Those scars, however, are a continual reminder to all of us that life is full of uncertainty and you had better not take anything for granted.

For a while after I left Tulane, I was afraid my goal of earning a Ph.D. would never be fulfilled. I had made three attempts at it, and, regretfully, the third time wasn't the charm the way it was supposed to be. I didn't go into deep depression over my unrealized goal, but I surely did have some serious regrets.

Partly to compensate for not being successful in my academic pursuits but more so because of my love for practical politics, I decided to make another race for the Mississippi House. That time, however, I would attempt to get myself elected to a post representing Forrest and Lamar counties. I convinced myself I was well enough established to have a decent shot at winning so I gave it a try.

My second race for the House was very different from the first in that I attempted to unseat an incumbent. I knew that would be difficult to do, but it was the only choice I had. The man holding the office was Bob Arrington, and he also had the advantage of being a lifelong resident of Forrest County. His advantages proved to be too much for me to overcome, and although I came close, I wasn't close enough. I brooded over my loss for several weeks but, fortunately, not long after that I heard about a new Ph.D. program in higher education that

Ole Miss was offering. What was new about it was the fact that the professors were making the courses available in Jackson as well as in Oxford.

After making a few inquiries, I knew that program would be almost ideal for me. With a college teaching emphasis I would have strong credentials for a career faculty position, especially at a community college.

Ordinarily, Ole Miss's requirement of 45 gradate hours in one's teaching field would have been a substantial hurdle, but with my courses from LSU, USM, and Tulane, I had already met the requirement. The only courses I would have to take for the degree were those in higher ed. In turn, that would mean if I took two of them each regular semester and one during the summer terms, I could complete all of the course requirements in two and one-half years.

Completely satisfied I'd found what I needed, I applied for admission early in '76. It was granted in plenty of time for me to get started in the program that summer. It was my plan to take each course I needed as soon as it was offered. That practice would enable me to get everything done in the shortest time possible. At the age of 36, I didn't want anything to slow me down. In my heart of hearts, I had set myself a goal of earning my Ph.D. before I became 40. That meant I had less than four years to take 12 courses in higher ed, meet the 12 semester-hour requirement in each of two foreign languages, pass the doctoral preliminary exams, choose a dissertation topic and get it approved, follow the myriad steps necessary to write an acceptable dissertation, and then finally defend that dissertation before a committee of professors from the department of higher education and several other departments. Just thinking about getting all those things done gave me a feeling of continuing apprehension. I had learned long before that most would-be doctoral recipients dropped out at one point or another along the way and I couldn't bear the thought of being one of them. With my history of being in and out of doctoral programs, I had met a number of those students. They would live out the rest of their lives with the ever-present knowledge they had tried and failed. Some of them got so far along they had done everything that was needed except writing and defending a dissertation. Ignoring the fear of what my fate might be, I got things under way. By a happy coincidence, my first Ole Miss professor was Dr. Robert Ellis. I took his course titled "The Finance of Higher Education" that first summer. From the moment he and I shook hands at the initial class meeting, I had the feeling my experiences with him would be good. Over the next three years, that feeling would be continually reinforced. I wound up taking three courses under him, and in each instance, he was well prepared, organized, interesting, and supportive. I worked hard for him and, judging by my grades, he felt I had performed well. In fact, on more than one occasion my performance on the midterm exam was held up as a standard for the entire class. I smiled and tried to look modest as he told my classmates they might take a look at my test to see the kinds of responses he was hoping to receive.

With college teaching being my emphasis, however, Dr. John Fawcett, the departmental chairman, was my major professor. As with Dr. Ellis, I quickly established a rapport with him and my class experiences were similarly gratifying.

The other professor who came down to Jackson regularly to offer courses was Dr. Katherine Rea. I had the pleasure of taking College Student Personnel under her. She had a knowledge of her subject second to none, and judging by my interactions with her, she respected my abilities fully as much as I respected hers.

With all of my classes meeting on Friday evening and Saturday morning, my usual pattern was to get to Jackson the best way I could on Friday afternoon and spend that night either with a family member or friend. Maureen and Bill lived close to the University Center where the classes met, so it was convenient for me to stay with them. By then, my nephew, Billy, and my niece, Lynn, were living elsewhere, leaving only Mary and Jay still at home. Thus there was plenty of room for me, and I stayed with them more often than anyone else. My friend, Jimmy Williamson, who had been my student assistant for two years while he was at USM, also lived close to University Center, and I stayed with him on a number of occasions, as well. Tom Kynerd and Lawrence Stacy, friends of long-standing, prevailed upon me to stay with them on numerous occasions because, as they said, that's what friends are for. I also stayed a couple of times with Bob DeVille, a friend from our Tulane days.

Getting to and from Jackson typically required a good bit of ingenuity on my part. I was embarrassed to continually have to bum a ride from one person or another, but for months that was what my circumstances required. Finally, however, another friend of long standing, Ann Jordan, from USM decided to enter the program, and my travel worries were largely over, except for the summers. Then, as I always could, I counted on Linda. I never showed up for a class unprepared either. Many of the friends who had read for me since 1961 were still around and, to my immense relief, were still willing to volunteer a few hours of their time to help me get my work done. More and more books on tape were also becoming available through an organization called Recordings for the Blind and Dyslexic. As a result, I could plan and execute my study schedule much more easily than I had ever been able to do. Contrary to the way it was with some of my colleagues, I never missed a class.

Because of the kindness and generosity of several students in the program from Southwest Junior College, my problems associated with note taking were also largely eliminated. The wife of one of them typed a verbatim transcript from recordings of the class that my professors always permitted. For a modest charge, copies of the notes were made available to any students wishing to have them. In the past, I had spent many hours typing my own notes from class recordings, but with this new opportunity, that time could be spent much more productively.

With Dr. Fawcett's permission, I took a couple of my higher ed courses at USM and transferred them to Ole Miss. One of them was Statistics, the very name of which left me shaking in my boots. Anything even remotely associated with mathematics always baffled me. I had to overcome that handicap, though, because I had to have credit in the course and at least a rudimentary understanding of the main concepts. Fortunately, my professor was Rex Leonard. Not only was he good in the classroom, he was even willing to take my phone calls and provide a little extra help. When I got my final grade, I declared to Linda that a "B" never looked so good.

There was also enough flexibility in Ole Miss's requirements to permit me to meet the foreign language requirements by using my USM courses. Though I had enjoyed studying both German and Spanish, I was delighted to not have to repeat the effort. Learning a foreign language was almost as difficult for me as understanding math.

Having been warned by several friends that writing a dissertation takes an unbelievably long time, I was on the alert for a possible research topic as soon as I started Dr. Ellis's course. Each time he introduced a new subject I examined it closely in hopes of discovering something that would spark an idea. I also began to read very widely, immersing myself in the literature of higher education, again with the hope of finding something that would give me a sense of direction. Week after week, I read and thought and hoped.

By late fall I had learned enough to know that college students' satisfaction was intrinsically interesting to me. Consequently, I read everything I could find on the subject, and eventually I stumbled upon an article that discussed a scientific measurement of student satisfaction through the use of an instrument called the "The College Student's Satisfaction Questionnaire." It had been developed by a couple of professors from Iowa State University who argued that a student's satisfaction with college could be measured scientifically in the same fashion that a worker's satisfaction with his job could be measured. After further reading, I learned that a doctoral student had used this new questionnaire as his research tool, and I began to think I might do likewise.

In succeeding weeks I discussed research possibilities with Dr. Fawcett and, eventually, settled on the idea of doing a study of student satisfaction at USM and perceptions of that satisfaction on the part of both faculty and high level administrators. For a period of time after I began the writing of my dissertation in the late spring of '77, I was enthralled with what I was doing and began to entertain the idea that I might be able to make a real contribution to my field. I told several of my USM friends as much, and they seemed to be in tacit agreement. One of them however, Joe Parker, a professor in Political Science, merely smiled and said, "Jim, the good dissertation is the one accepted by your committee."

For the next year and a half I had many occasions to recall Joe's advice. I revised my dissertation so many times to meet the demands of my committee that I lost count of the number. By the end of the process, I didn't much care what the dissertation said as long as my committee liked it. I just wanted to get through with it so I could get on with my life.

In the midst of all the work I did on my dissertation, I also had to make extensive preparation for my preliminary examination. This is a comprehensive examination that is designed to show that competence has been achieved in the various subfields of a student's discipline. Completion of the exam takes many hours and, as a consequence, it is as much a test of endurance as it is knowledge. When I finished, I was afraid my performance on a couple of questions would not be adequate and, to my deep embarrassment, that proved to be the case. Perhaps I had misinterpreted the questions or, worse yet, perhaps my preparations were inadequate. Whatever the case, I had failed to meet the challenge.

After redoubling my efforts and making sure on my second attempt I was so well prepared there was no way I could fail again, I went back up to Ole Miss and redeemed myself. The disappointment I had felt, which I was convinced was shared by my professors, was largely erased by my second performance. I marked it down as part of the process, but the memory of it never lost its sting.

In the spring of '79, Dr. Fawcett decided my dissertation was complete and that it was time for my defense of it. I was certainly ready to get it over with, but the prospect of having to appear before a committee and answer Lord knows what questions sent my spirits into a tailspin. My friends who had helped me along the way such as Don and Catherine Cotten and Bernard Pyle had done all they could, and from then on it was up to me. Catherine had even done a complicated mathematical analysis that appeared quite impressively, I thought, as an appendix to my dissertation, but I knew if anyone asked me about any part of her work, I would be sunk. I understood only the general concept. Any specifics that would be required of me would make me look like Ned in the primer.

When the time finally came in early summer for my defense, I was more nervous than I had ever been. In the final few minutes before I had to face my defense committee, if anyone had crept up behind me and said, "Boo," I would have jumped out of my skin. Fortunately, when we finally got things under way, Dr. Fawcett gave me an opportunity to settle down some by requesting I give the committee a brief autobiographical sketch. I thanked everyone for their attendance and then started talking about my life in Amite County and thereafter. Subconsciously, I might have been trying to take up as much time as possible, but whether or not that was the case, I must have overdone it because, eventually, Dr. Fawcett cut in and said, "All that's very interesting, but we better move things along." Then the questions began.

I was prepared for my defense to be something less than pleasant, but somehow I hadn't factored in the possibility of being offended by anyone on my committee. Unfortunately, I should have done so. The first person who spoke asked me a question that was so inappropriate I couldn't help but be offended by it. Sounding as if he thought his question went right to the heart of my research, he asked me why I had chosen the college students' satisfaction questionnaire as my instrument for collecting data rather than, as he said, one of the hundreds of others that were available to me. In actuality, the instrument I used was virtually the only one available to me and if he had carefully read my dissertation, he would have known that. Despite what was going on in my head, I put a smile on my face and tried to look merely interested as I attempted to give an appropriate response to an inappropriate question. The other members of the committee must have been convinced by my performance because no one followed the lead of the initial questioner.

To my dismay, however, the second speaker also gave me a jolt. What he did was to point out to everyone the fact that I should have used the term "stratified random sample" rather than simply "random sample" in referring to the technique I had employed in selecting the students who were to be a part of my study. I assured him, and all concerned, that I would certainly make that correction, but inwardly I was seething because the man making the recommendation was a member of my dissertation committee and a statistician himself. If his suggestion was really necessary, he should have made it to me on one of the fifteen or so occasions when he had the opportunity to do so.

After the rough start, things improved substantially, thank goodness, and I made it through the rest of the defense without undue difficulties. Dr. Fawcett was a strong leader, and he moved the process along as well as could be reasonably hoped. His ego, too, was involved in all that had happened as well, but, of course, he made a point of maintaining objectivity.

After an hour and twenty minutes, I was asked to wait in the departmental office while the committee made its decision. The time seemed to drag interminably as I sweated and paced. The departmental secretary tried to take my mind off of my misery, but I was inconsolable. Finally, after the longest ten minutes of my life, Dr. Fawcett came in and said I'd passed but that some changes would have to be made in the way I reported my data. Once again, the thought occurred to me that my dissertation committee member who had let me down a few minutes before had let me down much more seriously in the final stages of my work. Why, I asked myself, didn't he tell me weeks ago what I needed to do? Perhaps Dr. Fawcett was thinking the same thing, but neither of us said a word about what could have been done.

As soon as I got back to Hattiesburg, I started making the stipulated changes. By then, I had typed and retyped various parts of my dissertation so many times I had lost count. One more time won't make that much difference, I told myself as I typed in change after change, using the skills Mrs. Juanita Stevenson had taught me my senior year in high school.

Producing the rough draft with all of the necessary changes only took me two and one-half weeks because Dr. Fawcett was very explicit about what had to be done. He was also very prompt in accepting my changes and, very soon the document was in the hands of a professional typist. When her work was done and Dr. Fawcett had the finished product in hand, he called me and said, "Congratulations, Dr. Robertson." Those words were like music to my ears.

A very special thing occurred a month later when on August 8, my degree was officially conferred. I walked across the stage of the giant graduation arena with Linda at my side as my name was called. Pausing at the appropriate place, I stood still and solemn while the Dean of the College of Education, serving as the university's official representative, placed the appropriate academic regalia on my shoulders. The moment it settled into place, the audience of 5,000 erupted into loud and enthusiastic standing applause. Both in surprise and embarrassment, I listened as the sound thundered through the arena. Mistakenly, I assumed my family was responsible for what had occurred. Actually, it was not. The applause turned out to be a spontaneous response on the part of thousands as they saw what they perceived to be an especially worthy fellow receive the highest degree an institution of higher learning ever bestows. That knowledge made the whole experience even sweeter.

As it happened, I became the first person in my family to earn a Ph.D. In fact, up until 1937, no one in our family had ever even earned a college degree. My father bore the distinction of being the first to do so--a fact that gave him a sense of pride throughout his life. It would have been nice if had lived to see his son not only following in his footsteps but actually picking up the pace a bit. If Daddy couldn't be there though, at least Mama could. There was no doubt concerning how she felt about it. She didn't live her life through me or her daughters, but she always wanted us to be all that we could be, not for her, but for ourselves.

Soon after I returned home from Oxford, friends from all over began to call their congratulations. Two callers, my classmates Carter Lewis and Colleen Whittington Cameron, had both received their terminal degrees several years earlier. "That's not bad," I thought for a class of 50. We're about ten times above the national average. Just about where we ought to be. The people who had helped to make us what we were expected that of us. If we had not lived up to their expectations, they would have been disappointed in us, and we certainly couldn't have that to happen.

Chapter 13

Making a Move (GTT)

As I approached the age of 50, I became more and more concerned about being able to fulfill one additional important ambition. What I wanted to do was live and work in another state. I knew that if I didn't do it before I became 50, the chances of ever being able to do it would become remote. Thus in '87, after getting Linda's blessings, I began to look seriously for job opportunities.

Narrowing the search was fairly easy because I didn't think any of us would be completely content outside the South and I also didn't want to be too far away from Margie. Since she was on her own she wouldn't be moving with us, and I didn't want visiting to be a hardship.

Using the *Chronicle of Higher Education* as my chief source, I began searching for Political Science openings in all of the southern states. With my Ph.D. being especially well suited to community college teaching, I eventually focused completely on that type of institution. There are hundreds of these colleges throughout the South with Texas and Florida having two of the best systems found anywhere. Two of my friends from USM, Tyler Fletcher and Art Southerland, originated in Texas and still had enough ties there to be helpful to me as I found openings and began to make inquiries. With Texas being eight hundred miles wide and approximately that size from north to south, there is tremendous diversity within it from the standpoint of geography, culture, and climate. Though I ultimately decided that was the state to which I would like to move, I still could seriously consider only areas where I knew Linda, James and I would all have a good chance at being content. That meant the panhandle and large cities such as Houston, Dallas, and San Antonio were eliminated. Even so, a good number of possibilities remained and one of them, Grayson County Community College north of Dallas, asked me to come out for an interview.

My friend, Bernard Pyle, picked me up at the Dallas airport and gave me a ride to the college. I had an excellent meeting with the President of the college and the Dean of Instruction, but a much less successful interview with several members of the faculty. I handled myself fairly well, but the negative vibes I got from one faculty member in particular made me feel I probably wouldn't get an offer from that institution and my suspicion turned out to be accurate. Though mildly disappointed I felt, in general, I was better off than I had been before from at least two perspectives. First my experiences at Grayson County would serve me well in future interviews, and, secondly, I was spared the possible discomfort of being at an institution where at least one faculty member did not wish me to be.

Soon thereafter I learned of an opening at a newly established college just outside Mt. Pleasant, bearing the name Northeast Texas Community College. I sent those folk a copy of the curriculum vitae that my colleague, Sharon Evans, and I so carefully prepared, and, in a few weeks, good things began to happen. Bill Shafer, a good friend from USM, originated in northeast Texas and, better yet, knew some key people at the college. Among them were Jim Archer and Jerry Wesson, both high-level administrators. My personal experiences as a community college student and instructor, albeit briefly, plus my time in the Legislature and a Ph.D. grounded in college teaching caught their attention and that of the selection committee.

When I was called in for an interview, I could tell that the decision had largely already been made. Numbers of people at USM had been contacted, and obviously the people at Northeast liked what they had learned. As soon as I got on campus, Jim Archer took me in tow and introduced me to faculty and staff throughout the college. By the time I went in for the formal interview, I felt that what I needed to do was keep myself from looking stupid and the job would be mine. Fortunately I did just that, and, sure enough, a very attractive offer was made. To their credit, neither Linda nor James failed to give me their support in making what would be a life-altering decision affecting all of us. I sincerely believed it was a wonderful opportunity, and, thank goodness, I didn't pass it up. If I had, I would have spent the rest of my life second-guessing myself.

Among other benefits, being chosen as the only full-time political science professor at the college was a tremendous boost for my ego. According to Benton White, Selection Committee Chairman, there were literally hundreds of applicants, making the competition very keen. Most satisfying of all, I had been selected on the basis of my achievements and the good name I had made for myself in Mississippi.

Knowing we would truly be happy only if we found a church in which we were comfortable, we made it a point to stay in Mt. Pleasant following my interview long enough to visit Tennison United Methodist Church. It had been recommended to us by Jerry Wesson, and, from the very outset, we understood why. The people were friendly and open and very serious about the role of their church in the community and elsewhere. The minister, Jim Ross, was an excellent speaker, and the eleven o'clock service was fully as enjoyable as Sunday school.

On August 16, 1988, 24 years to the day after Linda and I had married, she, James and I left Hattiesburg to begin a new phase of our lives. My college friend, Nick Kolinsky, owner of a moving company, among other enterprises, transported our belongings without mishap and at a nominal cost. The rental house Benton White had found for us accommodated all of our things, and we spent a happy year in it before having to move to another one for a brief period. After that, we found a home we wanted to buy.

Shortly before we made our official move, Linda secured a teaching position in the Mt. Pleasant school system with the help of Carlos Kidwell, a newfound church friend. Her interview with Bob Cochran, Principal of Corprew Elementary, had gone extremely well, and she and I were both pleased about her professional future as well as mine. Establishing rapport with Bob Cochran had been easy, especially after he learned that my cousin,

Howell "Sonny" Huff, had been a quarterback of the football team when they had been students together at Louisiana College.

I feared that James might be unhappy in a completely new place, but, to my immense relief, he adjusted well. Randy and Sandra Hargrove and their sons, Heath and Justin, whom we also met at church, were very helpful to him as he began to get established. He also had the good fortune of being put in classes at Mt. Pleasant High School with teachers he thoroughly enjoyed. In his favorite subject, Social Studies, he had the pleasure of studying under Glenda Brogoitti, who later became a colleague of mine. He also had good experiences under Ms. Karen Blackwell and Mr. Jerry Fortner, despite the fact neither taught courses well suited for his interests and talents.

From the outset, I was quite pleased with my job and the other circumstances of my life. With Linda and me making substantially more money than we had ever made before, the quality of our lives and that of James as well was significantly enhanced. Being relieved of many of the pressures I had experienced before had a salutary effect on me, especially, and I was soon more contented than I'd ever been. Jim Archer had helped me get off on the right foot by calling on me for impromptu remarks at the college's first faculty meeting for the year. There are times when everything you do is exactly right, and that was the case when I stood and addressed all of my colleagues for the first time. I turned on charm that I didn't even know I had. By the time I had finished, the entire group was laughing heartily, and from that moment on, I was accepted as one of them.

A regular teaching load for those of us who were Humanities faculty was five courses. Typically, however, we were asked to teach one or more courses as an overload, for which we were paid, though not very well. In addition, we were expected to be in our offices and available to students for consultation at least ten hours per week. As a result, we all stayed extremely busy, and idle time was virtually nonexistent. Most of us took only a short lunch break and spent the rest of the time attending to our myriad responsibilities.

The courses for which I was responsible were American National Government and Texas State and Local Government. State law required all students to take both of those courses. Having taught American National Government countless times and State Government often enough to be comfortable with it, I entered upon my new responsibilities feeling quite competent. I had to learn some of the nuances of Texas politics as various course topics unfolded, but I was usually well prepared for each class.

The opportunity to attend college was an unfamiliar experience for the majority of our students. The community college district from which virtually all of our students were drawn was comprised of the counties of Camp, Morris, and Titus. The residents of those counties paid a special tax to support the college and were thus entitled to its services at the lowest-possible cost. Students from outside the district had to pay slightly more for the privilege of taking courses.

Because of the vision of Jerry Wesson, all Mt. Pleasant High School graduates entering college for the first time and taking a minimum of 12 hours were, and still are, entitled to attend college tuition free. Moreover, honors graduates have the additional benefit of having their textbooks paid for as well. Eligibility also requires, of course, acceptably high grades each semester. The cost of these benefits is underwritten by the proceeds from a one million dollar anonymous grant called "The Community Fund," which is administered by the trustees of Tennison United Methodist Church. The initial support Jerry got the trustees to provide in the mid-1980s has been continued every year since. What an extraordinary thing.

Over the years, additional funding sources for the other high schools in the district have been found so that now all graduates can attend the college tuition free. No doubt this makes Northeast Texas Community College unique among the thousands such institutions throughout the country.

With me teaching a large number of students each semester and immediately becoming a faithful member of one of the dominant churches of Mt. Pleasant, it wasn't long before I became fairly well known and a host of opportunities began to present themselves. Within a few months of the time we moved to Mt. Pleasant, I had brought the Laity Address at Tennison and had been the speaker at a meeting of the principle officers of Titus County.

Both talks turned out well, but the second took on a very unusual character. To my considerable surprise and complete enjoyment, one of the officials, Justice Court Judge Eva Laing turned out to be a sister to my friend, Butch Saunders, back in Amite County. I had just explained that I wasn't a native Texan, since I'd been born in Liberty, Mississippi, when from the back of the room Eva spoke up and said, "Yes, in Amite County." That helped me to further establish rapport with the group, and I wound up making a talk that was extremely well received. After the meeting, Eva and I visited and got caught up on one another the way Mississippians will always do.

The way life is, the joy and contentment Linda, James, and I were experiencing in our new home was bound to be interrupted, and it was. Actually it happened less than two months after we got to Mt. Pleasant, and it was one of the worst tragedies we could imagine. The death of family member is always a terrible and sad experience, but some are worse than others. We had suffered the loss of two babies in our family. Barbara and Robert's first child, Cherrie, and Linda Jean and Charles' fourth child, Kreg, but on October 15, of '88, we lost Bobby, Barbara and Robert's oldest son. I still grieve over the death of all three of them, but, since Bobby died well after he was a grown man, his loss continues to be the most painful. As bad as the pain is for me, his uncle, that which Barbara and Robert feel as his parents or that Janice and Larry feel as sister and brother, must sometimes be unendurable.

Even though I was still quite new at the college when Bobby died, the faculty and staff were very supportive of me, and I've always appreciated their generosity. By then, Jim Archer had returned to the classroom on a full-time basis, and Susan McBride succeeded him as our Dean. Susan immediately relieved me of my teaching responsibilities, and she and numbers of others helped me to make the necessary arrangements for Linda and me to immediately travel back to Mississippi.

Sandra and Randy Hargrove suggested we allow James to stay with them while Linda and I were gone, and we gratefully accepted their offer. The fact we had known them less than two months seemed to have no relevance. They saw an opportunity to help people in need, and they did what they felt should be done. As we would see later in many other instances, that's the kind of people they are.

As was the case with the Hargroves, many of the friends we made from the very beginning of our time in Northeast Texas were acquired through the church. Our experience had always been that the best people you can find will normally be people with strong religious convictions. That belief was confirmed many times over during the ten years we were Texans.

Of course, the church is important as well because it offers so many opportunities for service. Often, for me, the best service I could provide was that of presenting a Laity Address. I had done that on many occasions in Mississippi, and, knowing that, Jerry Wesson asked me to bring the message at my first Laity Day in Texas. I gladly did so, and, as it happened, it was one of many such addresses I made in the following ten years.

By the time Tennison was scheduled to observe Laity Day the following year, my position in the church was such that I was again asked to fill the pulpit. It was a responsibility I knew I should discharge, and I finally agreed to do so, but the closer to the day, the more nervous I became. Making any kind of speech always causes a certain amount of apprehension, but the one I was scheduled to make on October 15, 1989, was about to do me in. The problem was that my nephew, Bobby, had died on precisely that date the preceding year. I feared that during my talk I would break down and start crying because of the deep sadness I was feeling. I shared my fear with Linda, Margie, James and a number of friends, all of whom gave me their sympathy but nothing I did seemed to provide me with much relief. On October 8, when I made my weekly phone call to Mama, I told her what I was afraid was going to happen the following Sunday. As if she had known in advance what I was going to tell her, she said, "Well, you'll just have to brace up." When I heard those words, I knew she had given me the best advice that I could receive. She was a good role model for me too. She had been called upon to brace up many times in her life, and, by golly, she had done it.

As I sat talking with my friend, Sam Parker, just before time for him to get the service under way on Laity Day, I believed that I was going to be able to brace up, but I was scared. Just to be sure I had myself covered, I told him of my concern and asked him to be prepared to take over if that became necessary. I expected him to tell me that he fully understood what I was going through and that he could be counted on for whatever support I might need. Instead, he looked at me and said, "Dr. Robertson, you are a strong person. You have a strong personality and a great faith. You will get through this."

Although I had only known Sam for a short time, since he was my Sunday school teacher, I had come to understand him quite well. Like everybody else, I knew if Coach Parker said something was a certain way, that's the way it was. He was a hero to many people in Mt. Pleasant, including his wife, Norween, a highly respected person in her own right.

Things unfolded during my talk as I knew they would. I thought about Bobby several times and almost gave in to the sadness I was feeling, but I tamped down the pain and kept on talking. When I gave my closing prayer and sat down, I was absolutely exhausted, but my soul was at peace. At a time when I needed to do it, I had braced up. In my heart, I knew Bobby was proud of his Uncle Jimmy.

Over the years, I made so many talks at Tennison it reached the point where I felt I didn't have anything left worth saying. I shared that thought with my friend, Tom Nuchols, one day by telling him that I really only had two good speeches. To my chagrin, but to the delight of several other folk who heard him, he said, "Oh, well I must have missed both of them." Later, when I told Galand what a smart aleck her husband was, she said that she'd been trying for over 30 years to improve him. "Well, you're a miserable failure," I said. But Tom had still bested me, and I knew it.

Even so, my popularity as a speaker for various types of organizations grew, and I made a very large number of talks throughout Northeast Texas. A few of them were for money, but most of them were provided by me as a part of my service to the community. It was also good advertisement for the college, and I got a lot of personal satisfaction from being well received in virtually every instance.

I made it a point to get involved in various worthwhile community activities as well. Ultimately, two of them would capture the lion's share of my time and interest. They were Hospice and Habitat for Humanity. Among the many reasons those organizations were special to me was that they were also special to my friends, Jerene Sarratt and Leon Grissom. I wound up serving as the President of the Board for each of them, and in the instance of Habitat, I had the honor of being a founding member. Both Cypress Basin Hospice and Mt. Pleasant Habitat for Humanity continue to thrive, and I feel a deep sense of pride every time I think about them. Those organizations have a lasting effect on the lives of large numbers of people. That fact was brought home to me very vividly a short time ago when I was told by Tom Nuchols, who is still active in Habitat after all these years, that a son of Gloria Martinez, our first Habitat homeowner, had graduated from college as an engineer. My last memory of him was as a ten-year-old boy serving as an interpreter for his mom when Tom and I needed to discuss something with her. Perhaps the stability he enjoyed as a result of his family's having their own home played a role in his success. I like to think that anyway, and every time he crosses my mind, I smile.

Being gregarious by nature, I've always been a fairly public person, but during all of the ten years I was in Texas, that was even more true. Linda has never discouraged that tendency in me and, in fact, often found it quite enjoyable herself to be out and about. We both enjoy attending plays, for example, and since my colleague, Doug Hoppock, had established a wonderful reputation in the college's theater department, we immediately began attending his plays and continued that practice to the very end. By a happy coincidence, the first performance we attended was on December 2, 1988, which happened to be Linda's 47th birthday. I had told Doug in advance that we were coming and that it was to be a special outing for us. To my immense pleasure, he said he would mention that fact in his introductory remarks, and he was as good as his word. The attention we got enhanced our enjoyment of the evening and substantially increased the number of people who, very early, became familiar with the new family who had recently moved up to Northeast Texas from Mississippi.

Doug's kindness also nurtured my feelings of collegiality. Those feelings were strong from virtually the first time I set foot on the campus, and, happily, they persisted throughout my tenure. They were strengthened, in fact, in various ways. For example, every Friday morning quite a few of us gathered at a local restaurant for breakfast. All we did was eat heartily and share our thoughts and feelings, often in an outrageously amusing fashion. No one is funnier than a college teacher when he or she is in the right environment.

The sensitivity shown by my colleagues in helping me to do things I could not do for myself, such as drive to work every day, was also very touching for me. Though quite a number of them helped me from time to time, friends such as Benton and Christine White and Mel Griffin and Paula Wilhite drove me to work hundreds of times.

Not only did I have the opportunity for a close relationship with my colleagues, the compactness of our campus and other factors made it possible to maintain a close relationship with large numbers of students as well. For a few of them, those who worked as student assistants, even friendship became a possibility. I had such a relationship with all of my assistants who stayed with me long enough for us to get to know one another well. That was the case with James Armstrong, Scott Beggs, Terri Elliott, and Brian Huffines. With the exception of Brian, each of them, especially Terri, has made an effort to assure our friendship would continue. Brian did so as well until he succumbed to cancer. James and I had the privilege of paying our last respects to Brian at his funeral in Sulfur Springs, Texas. There was a sweetness to Brian's disposition that caused people to be drawn to him. Even though I only knew him for a few years, I still count him among the best friends I've ever had.

In succeeding years, numbers of other friends from Northeast Texas have succumbed to death. Among them are my good buddies, Ron Cowan and Randy Nobles from the college and, quite recently, Larry Thompson.

Inevitably, contact is lost with many old friends, but a few with whom I had a special relationship have made sure this did not happen. Jim Ross and Jessie Harris, both of whom were my ministers in my early Texas years, still check on me. Jim and his wife, June, did my family the great honor of travelling to Hattiesburg from Mt. Pleasant to attend Margie and Mark's wedding, despite the fact we'd only known them for two years. Sadly, our friend, June, did not live long enough to attend the wedding of James and Shannon, but, to her credit, Jim's lovely new wife, Karen, was there with him. Jessie and his wife, Virginia, have shown us similar kindnesses over the years as well.

Despite the considerable effort required to do so, several of our Northeast Texas friends have visited Linda and me in Hattiesburg. Fritz and Edna Acuna, James and Shirley Bowers, Doug and Lois Crawford, Tom and Galand Nuchols, Jim and Vicky Swann, and Dan and Ann Wickware have all given us the pleasure of their company and enriched our lives following our return to Hattiesburg in June of '98.

Though I think mostly about the friends I made during my Texas years, my mind often goes back to several major trips made by our entire family. In June of 1992, partly in celebration of James' graduation from high school and Margie's continuing progress toward earning a Ph.D., and, of course, for the sheer joy of it, all of us set out on a two-week trip to England and Scotland. After a few days in London, a world-class city in every sense of the term, we rented a car and began touring. Among other places, we visited Dover with its white cliffs and Canterbury with its remarkable cathedral.

On our way up to Scotland, we stopped and had tea in Alston, a town that is quite literally snowbound for a period of time each winter. A short time later, we crossed into Scotland and entered the area called the Borders, where Sir Walter Scott himself lived a few hundred years earlier.

Mark, who did all of our driving, surprised us the next day by taking us to a museum having a very close association with the Robertson clan. Despite his best efforts to prevent it, we got there very close to closing time, but the lovely lady who ran the museum, upon learning our names, said, "Oh, for the Robertsons, we will gladly stay open late."

Later we had the thrill of visiting Inverness and going to Loch Ness. Though the city has many attractions, the folk who are in positions of authority are obviously smart enough to know that Loch Ness naturally draws people because, although we are pretty sure there is no such thing as the Loch Ness Monster, there is still some room for doubt, isn't there? After all, no one has yet proven there isn't one.

From Inverness, we went to Campbelltown, and no doubt would have enjoyed it as well as all the other places we visited, but to the deep sadness of all of us, it was there where we learned of Mama's death. We all knew from the outset that such a terrible thing might occur, but Mama, knowing of our plans, had insisted weeks before that we make the trip. That's the kind of person she was. She always wanted us to do and be everything we could.

We managed to change all of our plans beginning on Sunday evening and make it back to Liberty on Wednesday morning for Mama's funeral. Quite a bit of sleep had to be sacrificed, but we arrived home in plenty of time. If I had needed any additional evidence that everyone in my family was of top quality, the sacrifices they made between Sunday evening in Campbelltown, Scotland, and Wednesday morning in Liberty, by way of Glasgow, London, New York, and New Orleans, would have been more than ample.

A couple of years later, we made another trip abroad, and, that time, we stayed a full two weeks. Mark largely made our itinerary for that trip, and having learned a lesson from before, we rented a seven-passenger vehicle for our touring. Very deliberately we went many places that most tourists wouldn't visit, often traveling on one-lane roads to do so. Remarkably, the occasional pull-over lanes made it possible to drive at a reasonable speed without feeling that you're taking your life in your own hands.

The high point of that trip for Mark was a visit we made to the Ferguson Clan's ancestral home. Our host, whose family had lived in the same house for over 400 years, was as charming and accommodating a fellow as could be imagined. Mark loved the whole experience.

Until we moved to Texas, we never had enough discretionary income for travel outside the United States. The timing of our move was also an important factor, of course, because Linda and I were getting into our most productive years when we made the decision to relocate. Regardless of the reasons, however, our improved circumstances during the Texas years made a number of things manageable that would otherwise have been difficult or, perhaps, impossible. We were able to buy a very nice home in Mt. Pleasant while continuing to own our home in Hattiesburg and barely notice the money we provided Margie as she attended college at USM. To her credit, however, it should be noted that she, very deliberately, covered most of her own expenses. She forced herself to take the ACT more than once so that she could get a high enough score to earn a nice scholarship. In addition, she performed well enough in all respects to be accepted to USM's Honors College, which paid a stipend. Feeling further responsibility for herself, she took a job on campus and earned additional money. Actually, with her tuition waiver because of my long tenure at USM, her direct college costs were more than offset by what was available to her purely through her own efforts.

Our improved circumstances also made it possible for Linda and me to provide Margie with the type of wedding she wanted. She and Mark married at Parkway Heights United Methodist Church on August 4, 1990, with all features of the service being exactly what she and Mark wanted. Linda and I very willingly covered every cost that was appropriate for us. Later, we even got my old friend, Nick Kolinsky, to transport all of their things up to Chapel Hill, North Carolina, so Margie could comfortably begin work on her Ph.D.

James was the beneficiary of our improved circumstances as well. We were able to buy him the Mustang GT he wanted as soon as he became a licensed driver. Like Mark, James believed no other car could compare to a Mustang.

James had planned to move back to Hattiesburg and live in our home, along with his Grandmother McSwain, as soon as he graduated from high school, but in another of life's unfortunate twists, she died before this move could occur. Thus, in less than a year, both Linda's mother and mine were lost to us, and Margie and James no longer had a grandparent. Linda's dad had died in 1982, but not before James and Margie and several other grandchildren had experienced the joy of that grandparent's love.

Despite the fact he couldn't have the pleasure of his grandmother's company, James elected to move back into his old home in Hattiesburg anyway, so he could continue our family tradition of attending USM. For a short period, he had a housemate, but for most of his college years, he had an entire house to himself. Linda and I visited often, of course, as did Margie and Mark when they could, but the rest of the time James kept the home fires going by himself. Like his older sister, he managed things quite well and called upon his mother and me for very little. He worked on campus to provide himself with spending money and cover some of his living expenses as well. Like his father and his sister, he also majored in Political Science and proved to be an excellent student. Also, as Margie had done, he spent part of a summer studying in Great Britain. Finding that time abroad to be quite worthwhile, he decided less than a year after graduation to return to Great Britain as a participant in a combination work and travel program.

By a happy coincidence, Linda Jean and I had the same spring break while James was abroad and, knowing we'd likely not have such an opportunity again, decided to spend the better part of a week in his company. Traveling by train, we saw some great sights together, both in England and in Scotland. A few days after Linda Jean and I arrived, a recently acquired friend of James' named Shannon Sherman joined our little group. From the outset, it appeared she and James were well suited for each other. In succeeding years, that observation was confirmed many times over.

Even though James took good care of our Hattiesburg home, by the mid-'90s the time had come for improvements to be made. Linda and I knew we would be living in it again before very long. It seemed reasonable to have the work done before our return. Having James available to oversee everything and lend an occasional hand assured that the final product would meet our expectations.

With a newly renovated home awaiting us, Linda and I decided to return to Mississippi at the end of our tenth school year in Texas. By then she would be able to receive retirement benefits from Texas and, after four additional years of teaching, from Mississippi as well. In my case, I had been receiving retirement benefits from Mississippi since 1989 and would be eligible to receive benefits through the Texas optional retirement program anytime I chose. Moreover, I would have the additional benefit of free insurance coverage for the rest of my life.

Even though there were many reasons for us to return to Mississippi, it was still difficult to leave Texas. Linda's Aunt Violet and Uncle Jack Fuller and their children, Keith and Carolyn, had made us feel welcome there as had hundreds of friends. It would be especially difficult for me to leave because it was in Texas where I felt I had really come into my own, particularly in my professional life. That process had begun even in the early days when Susan McBride was our Dean under Mike Bruner, but it accelerated several years later when Doug Crawford succeeded her under the presidency of Charles Florio.

As June of 1998 approached and the time for our departure was nigh, the many friends we had made began to show us even greater kindnesses than we had earlier enjoyed. Our Sunday school class gave us a memorable farewell party and topped it off with a lovely keepsake.

Shortly thereafter, some of my good buddies from the college treated me to a farewell meal at my favorite restaurant, Two Senoritas. Those who had known me from the first day I set foot on campus such as Jim Archer, Winston McCowan, Doug Richey, and Dan Wickware, stoutly denied having had any influence over what I had become. They claimed, quite rightly I think, that their shoulders were not broad enough to support that kind of weight. Other friends who were present such as Gerald Clark, Ken Hanushek, Tom Lynch, Larry Thompson and Jim Swann were similarly charitable in their remarks about me, and never once during the evening did they allow me to have a serious thought. Knowing me as they did, they knew they'd better keep me laughing.

Just before Linda and I, with the indispensable help of Terri Elliott, got everything packed up and ready to move, our good friends, Art and Jane Scharlach, held a dinner in their home in our honor. Several mutual friends rounded out the group in attendance, including Pete and Nancy Hairston, the only other native Mississippians Linda and I had met in Northeast Texas. We had an excellent meal prepared by both Art and Jane and spent as enjoyable an evening as could have been imagined.

James came up with his friend and former fellow employee at Movers and Shakers, Shannon Merritt, to get everything loaded on the moving truck and then rode home with Linda and me on June 11. Our ten years in Texas had been a very good experience for all of us but especially me, I suspect. I was leaving with a conviction I was a more well-rounded person than I had been, and, in some ways, I felt I was also a better man.

Though distance and other factors would prevent personal visits with our Texas relatives, it was my hope that phone contact would prove to be a reasonable substitute. Thankfully that has proven to be the case. Linda and I talk regularly with her Aunt Violet and her cousin Keith and occasionally with her cousin Carolyn as well. Maintaining a close relationship with Linda's mom's relatives gives us a great deal of satisfaction since family connections have always been important to us.

Chapter 14

Helping Others Realize the Dream

of Home Ownership

Once I had gotten myself completely resettled when Linda and I returned to Hattiesburg after our ten years in Texas, I got reinvolved in the work of Habitat for Humanity. With friends, such as Marvin Morris and Buck Ford from Parkway Heights United Methodist Church being active members of the Board of the Hattiesburg Chapter, that was very easy to do. When they learned I had been a founding member of the Mount Pleasant Chapter and both Vice President and President of its Board, they encouraged me to come and assist their efforts.

By the spring of '99, I was a member of the Board and an active participant in its deliberations. I never missed a meeting, and I wasn't shy about sharing my ideas. The Board was comprised of a good cross-section of Hattiesburg's citizens, and I was impressed with their level of dedication. A number of them had been serving on the Board for many years; their reward being the certain knowledge that what they were doing mattered a great deal.

In the fall, Buck Ford, President of the Board, appointed a nominating committee and charged it with the responsibility of recommending officers for the following year. Yvonne Ferguson, a banker; Marvin Morris, an attorney; Juruthin Woullard, an educator; and I comprised that committee. When our committee convened two weeks later, it became apparent that our choices were few. Virtually everyone who was even remotely viable had already served as an officer. In fact, it appeared I was the only one who hadn't yet had the distinction of having done his or her part. Thus, it didn't take a rocket scientist to see what was coming, but I didn't try to stop it. With the other members giving their full approval, Yvonne suggested I accept the nomination for President and she would take that of Vice President. In the ensuing discussion, all three gave their assurance of full support and I knew they would be as good as their word. Without serious hesitation, I assented, knowing that one of the most important prerequisites of leadership is merely being willing to serve. I had done it before and I could do it again.

When I began my term as Board President in January of 2000, our chapter was, on average, building one house per year. We all knew we should enhance our performance, but we were unsure of how to do it. Believing, as I did, that the more people we could have involved, the better off we would ultimately be, I set about dramatically expanding the size of the construction committee. For convenience, I served as its chairperson, and we started holding regular meetings. As I'd hoped, new life began to manifest itself. In various ways, we reminded one another that we were playing an important role in Habitat's goal of eliminating poverty housing. We proved that like Habitat's founder, Millard Fuller, we too could dream.

The family selection committee had recently chosen Herman and Audrey Smith and their children as the next home recipients, and it was readily apparent the choice was an excellent one. They very quickly showed they understood that they were an integral part of a great partnership and, perhaps as importantly, Herman proved to be both a skilled and willing worker.

With Habitat always being short of money and relying very heavily on volunteers for virtually everything we did, I had no alternative but to accept the reality that our progress would often be slow, but I still tried to move things along. My reasoning was as simple as Millard Fuller's – the faster a home can be built the sooner the next one can come on line as well.

Quite naturally, Saturdays were our most productive days, but we tried to make Monday through Friday count as much as we possibly could as well. Soon, we were able to meet this object by having a small cadre of workers help Herman with the work every weekday afternoon when he came in from his job.

When he walked on the work site at 2:30 p.m., Ray Andrade, Bill Ferguson, and Bud Weaver were there to meet him. After deciding on the principle areas of concentration for each of them, they set to work and stayed there until 5:00 p.m. This group also did much of the planning for Saturdays as well.

William Conner, a city employee with a strong background in construction, normally served as site supervisor on Saturdays, and very soon our progress could be seen each of the six days of our workweek. Herman proved himself to be the hardest worker anyone could imagine and the one willing to spend the longest hours. Herman was often still on the job at 2:00 a.m.

With excellent publicity being provided by the *Hattiesburg American* and WDAM Television, our community support increased substantially. Among many other groups, the USM Student Habitat Chapter became very heavily involved, and with this group came an increase in enthusiasm that was very contagious.

With many things falling into place as they did, we finished the Smith's house in September and began construction on number two in October. The partner family for that project was Tanya Britton and her children. Since things had gone so well on the Smith home, it looked as if we might be on a roll that would carry us well into the future. In many ways, that was precisely what occurred.

Toward the end of 2000, Marvin Morris and Yvonne Ferguson among others decided it was time for our chapter to have an executive director and that I should be the one to hold that position. As I learned later, virtually everyone else on the Board was in agreement. When I was told about what had been decided, I felt I had no choice but to concur. There was no way I was going to disappoint the people who had shown faith in me.

When Yvonne assumed the Presidency of the Board in January of 2001, I assumed my new responsibilities. She and the entire Board made it abundantly clear to me that I was expected to play an integral part in their goal of improving all aspects of our work. I took them at their word and immediately set out to do just that.

For the next five years and nine months, my life very largely revolved around my work. As the only paid employee, all aspects of our chapter's efforts involved me. I understood the inevitability of that happening and I did not attempt to prevent it. I always knew that if I no longer wanted those responsibilities, I could resign. As long as I held the position, however, I knew I needed to spend whatever amount of time was required to get the job done. Typically that meant I had a six-day workweek with a number of things being done on Sundays as well, even after the Board hired Rhonda Torres to handle our accounting needs and serve as my part-time assistant.

In my tenure as Executive Director, I had the pleasure of working under Board presidents Yvonne Ferguson, Shannon Williams, and Randy Henderson all of whom were very capable leaders. The same evaluation could be given to our Board members and several volunteers, especially Bud Cervantes who spent countless hours finding building sites.

Until late August of '05 when Katrina struck, I was generally content with my job though beginning to experience some fatigue. By then, we had increased our home production to three or four per year. For the most part, Habitat International was pleased with our performance though there was always a certain amount of pressure for us to do better.

As long as Habitat was under the leadership of its founder, Millard Fuller, a dependable set of values guided the organization. As is always the case, however, the only thing that you can absolutely count on is that things will change, and change they did. Ironically, not long before Katrina struck, Millard was ousted from his position as the head of Habitat and, by court order, forbidden to have anything further to do with the organization.

With the destruction wrought by Katrina, it was probably inevitable that Habitat would be thrust in the forefront of the reconstruction effort. Money poured into Habitat's coffers with the expectation that many homes would be built and that no time would be wasted in the process.

Though Hattiesburg was not hit directly by Katrina, enough damage was done here so that we were targeted by Habitat International for special attention. In a few weeks, we were given to understand that we were expected to very dramatically increase our production and, as we were assured, there would be resources aplenty to enable us to do so.

That same kind of pressure was exerted everywhere Katrina had left its mark, and soon there was a virtual construction frenzy involving a large number of chapters. Changes occurred so fast in Habitat's offices and functions it became impossible to keep up.

For several months after Katrina, I tried to tell myself I could accept all of the changes that were occurring, but I wasn't having much success at it. I tried to get in step, but it was awfully hard.

Finally, in the spring of '06, I accepted the reality that I couldn't change along with Habitat. I was too much of the old school. Thus, it became my firm conviction that I wasn't the person who could help lead Habitat in the new directions it would have to take. And as a result, I saw no alternative but to resign. Randy Henderson and the other Board members were kind enough to suggest I should not do so, but by then, I was very firm about my decision. I felt I was doing the right thing for Habitat and for myself as well.

After an extensive search, in which I was intimately involved, my successor was found, and, in September of '06, I was able to resign in good conscience. It was time for me to focus my attention on other activities. Since then, both Habitat and I have moved along quite well and, I have noted with pleasure, that many of the fellows with whom I worked so closely, such as Ken Williamson, Mike Pascarella, and Glen Newell, are still out there helping do Habitat's good work.

Chapter 15

Living the Life of a Writer

In 2002 I began work on my first novel. Two years later it was published, and I felt entitled to begin calling myself a writer. Novel number two is now virtually complete, and I've made a good start on a third. Each is set in the land that I know and love, and with more than a little pleasure, I shall refer to them as my Amite County Trilogy.

When I am working hard at my writing, I typically arise at about 2:00 a.m. That is the time of day when I am at my best, and after I've fortified myself with a pot of Community coffee and a couple of pieces of cheese toast, I am as creative as I ever get. Some days I will work hard for as many as five hours, virtually without stopping. Usually, however, I will spend about two hours that can be classified as productive. Occasionally, there will be a day when I write ten pages that are worthy of being kept. On most days, though, a good page or two is all I can muster. I am typically content even with that much, because over a period of months, a manuscript of book length will emerge.

For me, the enjoyable part of ultimately producing a book is in the initial draft. That is when the real creativity occurs and when the feeling of satisfaction is at its height. The problem, of course, is that the initial draft is never worthy of publication. It has to be corrected, edited, rewritten, fretted over, and often changed so completely that it barely resembles its original form. All of those efforts are far from being fun. They involve work and, invariably, a great deal of frustration. At times the inherent discomfort involved in all of it is enough to cause me to decide the whole idea was a bad one in the first place.

On the days when nothing goes right, I can sometimes alter the headlong lurch toward oblivion by remembering how I felt when my first novel took shape. The experience was so unusual, if it had not been mine, I would have questioned its authenticity. Its brevity alone would be enough to give strong evidence that there must have been something else involved. For anyone who would be inclined to think along those lines, all I can say is "Well, when the ideas started coming, it just didn't take very long for them to line themselves up in the right order." In well under two minutes, a book was formed in my head. Regretfully, the unfolding of the initial ideas and the obligation to ultimately tell the story the way it needed to be told would require an additional two years.

In the hundreds of hours I've spent working on books since I initially declared myself to be a writer, I am confident I have improved my style and enhanced the quality of the final product, but those advances only serve to uncover countless other areas where serious attention is needed. I try to console myself in the knowledge that even great writers go through the same struggles I do, but adopting the language of perhaps the best writer of them all, I find there is "cold comfort" in it.

Happily for me, all of the experts agree on one fundamental truth where writing is concerned. To a person they assert the necessity of knowing what other authors have done. At this stage in my life to be required to spend much of my time immersed in great literature, through the use of Talking Books, could hardly be classified as anything other that a welcome assignment. Spending long cold evenings or long hot days for that matter seeing how Steinbeck, Tolstoy, McCullough, or Welty can tell a story always gives me a sense of gratification. In such an experience, it is almost as if the author is there with you guiding you along so that you won't miss anything. On occasion, he or she will give you an advance warning that something profound lies before you, but in other instances it will unfold so quickly and with such force that you will say, "Well, I declare."

Spending all that time reading will also give you the excuse of reliving the joy of being a child. You can go back and read *Huckleberry Finn* or *Tom Sawyer* again and laugh out loud at their outlandish behavior. If someone hears you and asks what has happened, you will likely reply, without embarrassment, that you're laughing simply because you want to. You are under no obligation to explain further.

Even if a very different emotional nerve is touched, and you're sitting there crying when someone comes in and asks what has happened, you may still feel as if things are the way they ought to be. Tears, too, can have a salutary effect on the soul. If I can feel deep sorrow over the plight of Huckleberry Finn, an orphan boy conjured up out of the imagination of Mark Twain, perhaps I will be moved to do something about the thousands in Africa and elsewhere who must live every day of their lives without the protection of a mother or a father.

On those days when I feel the need to escape from a reality that is pressing down on me, I will find something light to read. Perhaps I will choose an author with no reputation at all and just let her carry me along as she uses pretty words to tell a story I've heard a thousand times before but can still enjoy. Or perhaps I will choose a western and let Zane Grey or Louis L'Amour prove, once again, that courage matters and that, ultimately, good will triumph over evil.

Spending long periods of time reading invariably has a number of positive consequences. In aggregate, they almost always result in a certain peace of mind. I may begin a book with something nagging at me, but soon that thought slips away as a different part of my mind begins to react to what the author has created. Remarkably, this will occur when I'm not reading fiction.

When my mind is released from the shackles of worry, it becomes free to roam about and land on whatever it chooses. That is when creativity will occur. All of a sudden, coming from Lord knows where, an idea will emerge and from it, with a little luck, others will follow.

For me, it's all highly unpredictable, however. I might overhear a commonplace conversation between two strangers and think of a way to get one of my characters back under control. Or, perhaps, I'm walking out to my mailbox with nothing in particular on my mind, and a piece of dialogue essential to the development of my story will occur to me. If I am really lucky, the path I need to take might even be found when I'm asleep. In such an instance, my conscious mind will take over where the unconscious one left off, and as soon as I awaken, I will know what I need to do.

Often, however, I just have to keep working at it until I get it right. Regretfully, there is no substitute for effort. Ultimately, all of that work will result in a finished product, but there is no way to predict how long it will take. Until the end is reached, there is nothing to do but keep moving toward it.

When the book is finally published, there will be a tremendous feeling of relief, but there will be a number of other rewards as well. There is, for example, the knowledge I have produced something that will surpass my own existence. For generations to come, there will be a reminder that I was here and that I left some evidence to prove it.

In the meantime, I have the pleasure of talking about what I have done. Typically, I will have to help create opportunities where I can discuss my writing, but there are times when I am asked to do so with no inducement whatever from me. That occurred recently when Maureen's classmates asked me to attend their reunion. Knowing it would be an enjoyable experience for Barbara Ann and Linda Jean as well, Linda and I invited them to accompany us. The session went extremely well, and, at its conclusion, we could say in confidence, "An enjoyable time was had by all." Maureen's friends, such as Eva Frances Dickson, James Allen and Pat Causey, Kenneth and Flora Nell Gordon, Rachel Martin Vigneault, Lora Emma Brady Dunn and numbers of others including our cousin Hewitt Tynes, said it was so.

Another memorable opportunity to talk about my writing occurred shortly thereafter when my sister Ann invited me to bring the program at her Rotary Club meeting in Jackson. My brother-in-law, Jim Somers, and family friend, Maxine Freeman, helped to swell the ranks of those in attendance, and once again, I easily established rapport with my listeners. No doubt the groundwork Ann had done by telling her fellow Rotarians about me helped to make the audience receptive. Regardless, the whole experience could hardly have been any better.

Though much of my life revolves around writing, I still find enough time to be involved in other activities that are of interest. As always, I support my church and its many functions, but I make it a point to not neglect secular institutions such as those attempting to protect our environment.

As always, I also spend as much time as possible visiting with my family. The death of my sister Maureen in 2002 serves as a continual reminder that the rest of us had better take every possible advantage to be together. My remaining four sisters and I get together as often as possible, and I visit with my nephews and nieces when the opportunity presents itself. With the exception of my nephews, Tim Mauldin in Massachusetts, and Kevin Carruth in Jacksonville, Florida, the children of my sisters live close enough to permit an occasional convenient visit. One of my nieces, Mandolin Mauldin, is in the unique position of having both me and an uncle on the other side of her family with whom she can visit when she is able to come to Forrest County.

Since air travel out of Hattiesburg is convenient, Linda and I are able to go up to Indianapolis to see Margie and Duncan any time we wish. Being with them now is more important than ever because on February 12, 2008, Mark finally lost his fight against cancer. My role as Duncan's grandfather is also now more important than ever.

Margie has recently become the Chair of the Political Science Department at Indiana University Purdue University Indianapolis, a position which she finds both rewarding and challenging. Obviously her Ph.D. from the University of North Carolina, which she was able to earn in only six years, is serving her well. Duncan has a good school situation and as always is loved by every one who gets to know him.

James and Shannon have been living quite happily in New Orleans since 2005 and plan to be there for the duration. James is a supervisor for Advantage Sales and Marketing and Shannon is a Registered Dietician with University Hospital. They are in the enviable position of actually enjoying what they do. With Hattiesburg and New Orleans being only one hundred miles apart, both weekend and day trips are quite manageable.

Spending time with friends is also a joy, of course, but even after more than forty years of marriage, Linda and I prefer to spend most of our time in one another's company. We have found that there is no substitute for the shared memories of life, especially those that are happy, but because of their inevitability, even those that are unhappy. With the help of one another, we were able to bear up under the deep sadness of Mark's death and provide some support for Margie and Duncan. Perhaps we were also able to provide a little consolation for Mark's Mom, Evelyn.

Having just described the quality of my life as I approach three score and ten and in previous chapters having discussed various other aspects of my life, it now seems appropriate to do a little summing up. In my family we like to think that "We've amounted to something." That's our way of asserting that we've been successful and I confess that I have sometimes been guilty of giving myself that label. Fortunately, I also have an occasional experience which reminds me that if we are not careful we'll put too much stock in our success. One of those experiences occurred recently at Parkway Heights United Methodist Church when my friend Clint Gill was a guest minister for the eleven o'clock service.

Shortly before that day I had virtually completed the initial draft of this work and I was feeling a little more than satisfied with myself. Down deep I think I knew better than to entertain those thoughts, but even if I didn't, Clint clarified things for me quite well by saying "God didn't call us to be successful – God called us to be faithful."

In the face of such a self-evident truth I immediately gave up the idea that I might be a success. Upon further reflection, however, I settled upon a belief that I would hold on to with a high level of tenacity. It is the conviction that my family and friends are due most of the credit for me becoming the person that I am. It is my hope that I have not been a disappointment to them. I have tried to live in such a way that I wouldn't have to explain what I have done. I wanted my life to be a declaration of my beliefs. If that has been so, things are as they should be and I can feel at peace, secure in the knowledge that those who care about me won't have to wonder if I am doing well. When they see me, even on my darkest days, I want them to say "He's not giving up – he's moving forward, trying to get beyond darkness."